Anton Voroniuk
Alex Polishchuk

CUTTING-EDGE DIGITAL MARKETING

How to attract customers and increase online sales

The Content

What the reader will learn from this book............ 8

Chapter 1. Introduction to Digital Marketing 9

Chapter 2. Formation of a Digital Marketing strategy.
    The main questions 12
- 2.1 Who am I? The mission and the value of your company 12
- 2.2 What do I offer? Product or Service 13
- 2.3 Where am I? Analysis of niches and existing competitors 13
- 2.4 Why go online? Establishing a key performance indicators (KPI's) system and setting up web analytics 14
- 2.5 Who is our client? Creation of a target audience's portrait - characters, personalities, avatars, etc… 15
- 2.6 What? Content types that are currently working 16
- 2.7 How to promote? Promotion and content seeding tools 16
- 2.8 Could it be better? Regular improvement 17

Chapter 3. Competitive analysis and assessment of opportunities 18
- 3.1 How bad is your website now? How much traffic do your competitors get, and from which sources? 18
- 3.2 How well is your website doing in search engines? ... 22
- 3.3 What content do your competitors create? 23
- 3.4 What type of content gets shared most on social networks? 23

Chapter 4. Web analytics - how to evaluate the result? 25
    4.1 The Role of Web Analytics in Digital Marketing 25
    4.2 Identify key performance indicators (KPIs) 26
    4.3 Conversion group 29
    4.4 Measuring conversions 35
    4.5 Web Analytics Tools to Improve the Site 41
    4.6 Web analytics checklist 42

Chapter 5. Portrait of the target audience. Forming a user persona 44
    5.1 Who is your client? 44
    5.2 Audience data from web analytics systems 45
    5.3 Audience data from social media pages statistics 46
    5.4 Audience polls 48

Chapter 6. Content 50
    6.1 Using blogs 51
    6.2 Video content 52
    6.3 Event Content 53
    6.4 Who's responsible for everything? 54

Chapter 7. SEO (Search engine optimization) 55
    7.1 SEO or paid advertising? 55
    7.2 On-Page SEO 57
    7.3 Link building and other factors 65
    7.4 Conclusions, cases, and recommendations 69
    7.5 SEO Checklist 72

Chapter 8. Paid traffic 76
    8.1 Benefits of PPC 76
    8.2 What does PPC advertising help with? 77
    8.3 Principles of PPC advertising 80
    8.4 Checklist for launching PPC 85

Chapter 9. SMM - Promotion in social networks 87
    9.1 Why go to social media? 87
    9.2 SMM pitfalls 89
    9.3 Social media promotion tools 95

Chapter 10. Email Marketing 102
    10.1 Where can I get a subscriber base? 103
    10.2 Email Marketing Checklist 108
    Case study 108

The authors of this book are the founders of Webpromo agency, one of the most prominent Google Partners in Ukraine. Mr. Polishchuk and Mr. Voroniuk have had experience building successful online businesses for themselves and their clients. I am confident that their experience will help entrepreneurs build an effective sales system on the internet.

Dmytro Sholomko,
CEO Google Ukraine

The WebPromo team are the top professionals in their field. I have known the founders of the company since 2010, and we have been working together for seven years. We have promoted projects in international markets and have obtained excellent results. The WebPromo team have proven themselves to be responsible and reliable partners. The knowledge they will share with you in this book will come in handy if you are an internet entrepreneur or a startup company.

Alexei Vitchenko,
CEO of Digital
Futureinvestment company

Anton Voroniuk is the founder of WebPromoExperts Academy. For over eight years, WebPromoExperts Academy has educated more than 9,000 people, and more than 200,000 people have participated in their webinars and online conferences.

Alex Polishchuk
Director of Effective Internet
Marketing at Webpromo

WebPromo is one of the leading internet marketing agencies in Ukraine and is a Google Premier Partner and a Facebook Marketing Partner. WebPromo has more than 200 small and medium-sized business clients. They also have several brand clients and corporate clients such as Johnson &Johnson, BNP Paribas, Bayer, Vodafone, The United Nations, OSCE, and others. The purpose of this book is to help your project attract new customers online. This book will be useful for business owners, project managers, and marketing specialists who were faced with a lack of audience, calls, and inquiries after their site launch.

If you want to attract new customers, build systematic digital marketing, and establish a strong brand and online community, then this book is for you.

What the reader will learn from this book.

After reading this book, you will have:

- A clear picture of your competitors' activity online.
- A set of tools to track your work's effectiveness, and you will be able to monitor what your team is doing.
- Understand how to attract customers from search engines, social networks, and mailing lists.
- How to form checklists and detailed guides for further independent work on your project.

Chapter 1
Introduction to Digital Marketing

Over the past few years, the internet has taken a position as a must-have tool for promoting a business of any size. Nowadays, you can find people of any age, interest, and income on the internet. Every company tries to be present online, and this has led to an increase in competition. Since there are more content and advertisements on the internet, the customer acquisition cost has begun to rise, and it will continue to do so.

We help businesses increase their online customer flow by providing promotion services and training for entrepreneurs and their employees. The main thing you have to deal with in digital marketing is the lack of a system. This book was designed to take individual tools and bring them together to function like a well-oiled machine. We will be asking you questions, and you, dear reader, will be answering them. As a result, when turning over the last page of this book, you will have a full understanding of:

- Who your online competitors are and how they are achieving success.
- How to measure results.
- What key performance indicators to use and what tools are required to fix them.
- Who your client is online and how to communicate with them.
- What content is needed to attract and retain a visitor.
- Which traffic sources to use and how they work.

By reading this book, you will have a step-by-step system with which you can use to significantly improve your current business position, increase turnover, and possibly reach the top of your niche online.

We have been in the online promotion business since 2008. We are aware of how internet advertising strategy has changed over time. At first, the most common strategies were to use search query advertisements, SEO's, and then a little later on, PPC advertising in search engines. These tools are useful; however, the competition is increasing. The costs of online promotion are growing, and the efficiency of these tools is lessening.

Nowadays, it is necessary to use a systematic, integrated approach to online promotion; one tool on its own does not work. This book will tell you how to build an effective digital marketing system and focus on your customers. We will also teach you how to use the main promotion strategies.

The case studies used in this book are from our practice, our clients, and our students from the WebPromoExperts Academy. In 2008, when opening an online marketing agency with our partners, we 100 percent believed in a simple advertising model. Long story short, it worked, and clients started finding us by using search engines and by typing in search requests like «website promotion,» «website advertisement,» and «SEO optimization.» We were first everywhere, whether it was in organic search results or paid advertising. Customers saw this, and the inflow was quite strong. If you were a company in the B2B sector, you could get 20-30 new contracts per month, which is an excellent figure. We were growing rapidly, and our service was simple and straightforward. In two months, we were at the top for almost every keyword search. At that time, SEO was magic. For 200 dollars, your website could rank at the top of any search engine. We could easily gain traffic and service requests, which was like music to our ears.

With the changes in modern algorithms, SEO has ceased to be magic, and it has become just another marketing tool. However, it still generates massive traffic and is relatively cheap. Paid advertising in search engines went from being a complicated afterthought to being an indispensable part of online promotion. PPC advertising gives advertisers a lot of really wonderful opportunities to interact with the most targeted audiences. The shift to paid traffic has led to an increase in competition and, as a result, in transaction costs. This has led to an enhanced emphasis on automation and measurability.

Social networks have always appealed to marketers because of their seeming simplicity. However, solving the problem of getting sales from a post is not that easy. True, social networks draw the same audience as search engines, but visiting these websites is different. If your product does not fit into the categories of leisure, communication, recreation, and networking, your path to success on a social network will be long and rough.

The simplification approach created the second problem with social networks. The simplification approach means measuring the likes, subscribers, fans, shares, followers, and views you get. What came out of all of this, you might ask? Flocks and hordes of bots started appearing across all social network sites to feed somebody's ego. There became many more fake accounts on social networks. Businesses online are no longer looking for a magic button known in our circle as a 'CTA button' or a 'Call-to-action button'.» The time has come for an integrated approach and multichannel strategies. To sell your product or service on the internet, you must be present simultaneously wherever your client is.

Content marketing has become the backbone that helps bring channels together and make them work in synergy. If any of this sounds intimidating, do not be worried! In this book, we will walk through all of this together. You will learn how to drive not just traffic but quality traffic to your website. This traffic will become your regular paying customers, who will come back to you again and recommend your product or service to their friends.

Chapter 2
Formation of a Digital Marketing strategy. The main questions

2.1 Who am I? The mission and the value of your company
2.2 What do I offer? Product or Service
2.3 Where am I? Analysis of niches and existing competitors
2.4 Why go online? Establishing a key performance indicators (KPI's) system and setting up web analytics
2.5 Who is our client? Creation of a target audience's portrait - characters, personalities, avatars, etc...
2.6 What? Content types that are currently working
2.7 How to promote? Promotion and content seeding tools
2.8 Could it be better? Regular improvement

Where to begin? If you want to market online, there are a few simple questions you need to ask yourself before you start. If you don't take the time to answer all of these questions, you will not get the results you want from your internet promotion.

2.1 Who am I? The mission and the value of your company

The mission of your company is the reason it exists. You should know your mission before starting your campaign because your mission will determine how you communicate online. Therefore, when creating your mission, it is vital to add things that will distinguish you from your competitors and help customers understand the value you bring. Creating your mission needs to be done before you use any marketing tools online or offline.

Our academy's mission is straightforward.

We help people to become experts in digital marketing.
Accordingly, our primary audience is entrepreneurs, marketers, and internet marketing specialists who want to increase their online sales on all channels. Think about what your company's mission is. If it is not yet shaped, try to think about what you want to communicate to your audience. You must come up with a good mission because it will be present on all your marketing platforms. Do not continue with your marketing campaign until you have come up with a solid mission.

2.2 What do I offer? Product or Service

The product phase is about answering the question of «what do we offer?» How your product is perceived is very important. People have to understand your product or service and how it differs from your competitors' products and prices. I recently conducted training for a company that sells dental equipment. When we started analyzing their competitors' advertisements, we saw a few interesting things worth noting. When we did a Google search for «dental equipment sales,» we found ten competitors with almost identical ads. The main message was, «our dental equipment is high quality.» I can hardly imagine at least one company that would describe its equipment as that of poor quality. From what I saw, there was nothing special about their unique sales propositions. From a product perspective, your unique sales proposition is extremely important. You want to stand out and be different from everyone else! Do not use generic USP's because this will make your product seem dull.

2.3 Where am I? Analysis of niches and existing competitors

Where does your company stand at this moment in the market? You must understand where you are in the market, what tools your competitors are using, and how they communicate with their audience. There are many tools available on the internet that allow you to see how much traffic your competitors get. You can also see what channels and sources this traffic is coming from and how your company stacks up with theirs.

One of the first tools that you should use is SimilarWeb.com. SimilarWeb can analyze all sites except for those with less than 50,000 visits per month. Other tools such as SEMRush.com, Serpstat, and Ahrefs can help you explore what your competitors are doing in keyword searches. If you want to gain a detailed insight into how your competitors perform on social media, use tools such as BuzzSumo, Ahrefs, and SemanticForce. You must conduct a competitive analysis before you start a promotion, generate content, or drive traffic to your site. As you can already see, they're many things that go into making a great campaign. If you have a good mission, a unique sales proposition, and an understanding of the competitive environment, you will be able to form a high-quality strategy for your project. If this seems like a lot to take in, don't worry; we'll go through everything in detail later on.

2.4 Why go online? Establishing a key performance indicators (KPI's) system and setting up web analytics

Analytics is the core of digital marketing. With the right approach, you can measure everything! But instead of measuring the things that affect your business (sales, requests, orders, calls), I typically see beginners measuring things that are just easy to measure. For instance, likes on social networks, tweets, and shares. You don't need to bother with these things. It would help if you focused on leads, calls, and orders that you can get from social networks.

Web analytics provide an understanding of which key performance indicators you need to pay attention to succeed. For example, a service like Google Analytics will analyze who your client is, what sources bring audiences to you, and which content works best. Once you have clearly defined the goals and indicators you will be measuring; you can now use Google Analytics to determine who your client is and what sources and traffic channels bring the most buyers to your website.

You must understand that the online decision-making process is long. For example: (see the image above) this is how our client decided to buy our course. We communicated with him through our newsletters, emails, search engines, etc... There was multichannel online communication. The goal here is to communicate with a person via multiple channels before he buys something from us. You must be prepared for multichannel communication. With the proper setup of analytics and measurement systems, you can find out and calculate all of this. Later on, in this book, we will explain what specific tools can measure inbound leads, calls, and orders and convert these requests to real sales.

2.5 Who is our client? Creation of a target audience's portrait - characters, personalities, avatars, etc...

Who are the people we want to target online? When a client comes to our agency, we ask them to describe who has a demand for their product and service. We usually get one of two answers. Some say that their audience is everybody (something like 'the product is good, and everyone needs it'). The second situation is a sort of fantasy scenario. For example: our client is «a 25-year-old man who drives a used foreign car».

To have a clear portrait of your potential client, you will need some expertise in a particular set of tools. This book will help you use specific sets of tools that are available for free or cost little money. These will help you get a clear picture of the people who want to visit your website and buy from your website. We can get specific in what we can find out about a potential client like their gender, interests, where they live, and what devices they use to access your website. You will find out how they consume your content, on what days, and at what time of the day. You will have a clear understanding of what needs, fears, and biases they have towards your product. This is all done with simple, straightforward tools, and you will learn how to apply them to your marketing strategy. Only after you have drawn a detailed portrait of your buyer can you start generating and creating content for them.

2.6 What? Content types that are currently working

We will learn how to address the needs of your buyer persona using content. We will discuss content strategies, but first, let's define what types of content there are.

- Professional, where you share your expertise.
- Specialized, which shows your understanding of what is happening in the market and where you are heading to.
- Personal, establishes you as a company and brand with a human face.

You need to choose the correct proportions for these components and transform them into text, video, and event content. Content is the core of all of your online marketing. It removes the audience's problem and allows you to build regular communication with the client and form a community around the brand.

2.7 How to promote? Promotion and content seeding tools

Once you've created your content, it's crucial to apply it correctly. Promotion tools will be traffic sources that respond to the generated demand. Search engine optimization, search advertising, and price comparison websites are the tools that will inform a person what your product and service is, even if they do not know about it yet.

Demand generation tools are banner advertising, video advertising, online public relations, social media advertising, and teaser ads. Tools that allow you to re-communicate with the person who visited your website are social networks, email newsletters, push-notifications, SMS, and remarketing tools (also known as retargeting). All these tools work cohesively as one unit to create great content for your product. We'll show you how to use these tools to promote your brand and increase your sales.

2.8 Could it be better? Regular improvement

Many entrepreneurs believe that the internet is a magic button; however, it is a standard business process to continually advance, improve your content and website, improve traffic and your decision-making funnel. You need to work to make these things better. Remember that these tools will allow you to start your online promotion properly.

Let's think back to chapter 1 for a second. There were eight questions that you had to answer to build a complete strategy. Assuming that you already understand who you are as a company and what customer value your product has, we will skip questions # 1 and # 2.

Let's start our journey with an analysis of the competitive environment.

Chapter 3
Competitive analysis and assessment of opportunities

Analysis of the niche and existing competitors

3.1 How bad is your website now? How much traffic do your competitors get, and from which sources?
3.2 How well is your website doing in search engines?
3.3 What content do your competitors create?
3.4 What type of content gets shared most on social networks?

3.1 How bad is your website now? How much traffic do your competitors get, and from which sources?

It is crucial to understand what your market position is and what the capabilities of your competitors are. This will allow you to set your goals correctly, start with the most effective traffic tools, and more. Competitor analysis services such as Similarweb, SEMRush, Serpstat, and others, give you an insight on critical points:

1. What kind of traffic can you attract to your niche?
2. What is the quality of your site compared to the sites of your competitors?
3. Where did they attract their traffic from?
4. What is their growth trend?

Let's start with the most powerful service available, Similarweb.com. SimilarWeb will allow you to see how much traffic your competitors have, the quality of your site's traffic compared to your competitors, and where your market peers are acquiring their audience.

Traffic Sources for amazon.com

On desktop

Figure 1 SimilarWeb traffic source data.

I suggest that we get started right away and move straight from theory to practice. Put your laptop in front of you and fill in a table with an analysis of your competitors.

№	Site	Visits	Time on site	Page/Visit	Bounce rate	Traffic sources
1						
2						
3						
4						
5						
6						
7						
8						
9						
10						

Put 10-15 competitor websites into your table and answer the three questions I set above. We will need SimilarWeb.com for this exercise. Just add your website to SimilarWeb.com, and then let's analyze this data together.

The following data has to be gathered:

- Audience size
- Monthly traffic
- Quality of the site
- Average time spent on site (Avg. Visit Duration)
- Average number of web pages (Pages per Visit)

- Bounce rate (percentage of visitors who viewed only one page of the website.)
- Main traffic sources
- Which sites drive the most referrals;
- A percentage split between paid and non-paid (organic) search traffic
- Major social networking sites
- Traffic trend over the past six months.

Important note! Similarweb will not present data for websites that receive less than 50 thousand monthly visits. Before starting any activity, it is vital to understand whether there is a significant number of audiences in your niche.

The size of your competitor's audience is the first thing you need to pay attention to. Paying attention to your competitor's audience's size will allow you to set accurate expectations of possible traffic volume in your niche. Some niches have a traffic volume of more than 10 thousand visitors per month, others have more than 100 thousand visitors per month, and there are even niches with more than a million monthly visitors. Analyses of sites like Amazon and eBay show that their monthly audience exceeds a billion. An objective understanding of how much traffic your competitors get will help you build realistic plans and move towards achieving what you want.

Site quality - Similarweb gives us three simple audience engagement metrics:

- Average time spent on a site (Avg. Visit Duration)
- The average number of web pages viewed (Pages per Visit)
- Bounce rate (percentage of visitors who viewed only one page of the website)

Compare your site to your competitors using these three metrics. If you are significantly behind your competitors, then you need to improve. It is important to consider the type of website you are viewing. They should all be similar. You cannot compare a full-fledged online store with a one-page website... Remember this!

The issue of the website's quality is extremely subjective. Usually, it is one person in the company who makes the final website development decisions. This is either the director, marketing director, or marketer. His taste preferences will determine whether the design will be restrained or lurid or if the developers try to fit all the information on one page instead of making a full-fledged website.

When I ask large audiences if they consider their site to be of high quality, only a few hands are raised. Dozens of hands raise when I ask if their website is of low quality. But these are examples of subjective opinion. A website that may seem like an outdated monster to you may fully correspond to your audience's user experience. This chapter's main idea is to make objective data-driven assessments rather than rely on a certain person's opinions.

Competitors' traffic sources
You have already been «inspired» by the traffic volume on competitive sites, but now you are tormented by the questions - 'how they are getting traffic?' and 'where from?'. Let's take a closer look at precisely what sources your market colleagues are getting their audience from.

An example of different traffic sources:

Let's comment on each of these columns.

Direct (direct traffic) - the audience that knows how to spell your website's name and enters it directly into the browser's address bar or arrives at the site through browser bookmarks. This is your loyal audience!

Referral (referral traffic) - traffic that came from backlinks (links from some other websites) - partners, dealers, forums, news resources. Scrolling down the report page, slightly below, you will see the TOP 5 referrers.

Search (search traffic) - this includes referrals from organic search results and paid search ads.

Social (social traffic) - traffic from social networks.

E-mail (email traffic) - traffic that comes from your email marketing campaigns.

Display (display advertising traffic) - traffic from banner ad networks.

Competitive analysis is extremely useful for both startups and already existing businesses. For example, we saw that our competitors' search traffic dynamics are higher than ours over the past year, even though we are doubling in size year after year. This has led to a shift in SEO strategy and a nearly 50% improvement in search traffic dynamics. That concludes our acquaintance with SimilarWeb; now, we will move to competitive analysis in search engines.

3.2 How well is your website doing in search engines?

Search is the leading driver of traffic in most niches. There are 10 billion Google searches per day. These people are looking for services, products, information about companies, and solutions to their problems. Understanding the strategies of search traffic is just as important as understanding the general state of affairs.

You need to know:

- Keywords your competitors use in search engine optimization
- Keywords your competitors are using in paid ads
- Messages that are used in ads
- which pages of a website drive the most traffic
- The main competitors in organic and paid search advertising

You can find out all of this information using services such as SEMRush and Serpstat. The one you use depends on the geographical location of your business. Each of these tools is easy to use. You enter a website address or a key phrase, and then you get detailed information about how to improve your search engine optimization marketing.

3.3 What content do your competitors create?

It is extremely important to sit down and review your competitors' activities regarding their content strategy. So what should we do? Re-read blog posts and review videos on YouTube-channels?

I would recommend that you do some of the things below instead:

- subscribe to the mailing lists of your major competitors.
- follow their social media profiles.
- subscribe to their YouTube channels.

3.4 What type of content gets shared most on social networks?

Social networks have a vast audience. People go there to communicate, have fun and, of course, share information. How often have you seen posts like «Recommend a dentist ...», «Which cheap Android phone is better?», etc...There is traffic on social networks, and high-quality content is the primary way to drive traffic from there. Understanding which content will work and which will not work is extremely important.

Tools like Ahrefs Content Explorer and BuzzSumo let you know what content gets the most social media shares. It's crucial to realize trends that are going on within social media. So how do you use this newfound knowledge? Well, take me for example. When I was preparing the next annual content plan, I noticed that our market peers get the most reposts from compilations of:

- top blogs
- top Telegram channels
- top YouTube channels worth subscribing to

The advantage of such compilations is that they can always be expanded, regrouped, and supplemented with your comments, and you get an excellent viral post. A blog post of TOP 500 Digital Marketing Blogs has garnered more than 1500 reposts and is one of the five most-read blog posts.

Competitive analysis is a regular process. It should be done at least once a quarter or at least once every six months. Doing competitive analysis will allow you to distance yourself from the competition and always be ahead.

Chapter 4
Web analytics - how to evaluate the result?

4.1 The Role of Web Analytics in Digital Marketing
4.2 Identify key performance indicators (KPIs)
4.3 Conversion group
4.4 Measuring conversions
4.5 Web Analytics Tools to Improve the Site
4.6 Web analytics checklist

4.1 The Role of Web Analytics in Digital Marketing

Web analytics is the pulse of digital marketing. Everything is measured, and everything is measurable. With Google Analytics and a call tracking system, you can clearly understand who your client is, how to improve your site, and which traffic sources are the most beneficial for your business.

In the first chapter, we said that the ideal process in digital marketing consists of several stages:
1. Understanding the company's mission and product
2. Understanding the product and its USP
3. Competitive Analysis
4. Goals and KPI
5. User persona
6. Content Generation
7. Attracting traffic
8. Analysis and optimization

Almost every step of the way, analytics is necessary.

4.2 Identify key performance indicators (KPIs)

It is very important to understand the indicators given by online advertising at each possible stage. When you ask a business owner what metrics they would like to use to measure promotion results, you will probably hear something like «sales.» In truth, transactional analytics brings together web analytics, a CRM, and an accounting system that tells us how well a promotion is doing.

Before we get to sales, you need to go through a fairly long chain of metrics united by Key Performance Indicators (KPI).

When building a KPI system, it is worth highlighting three groups of indicators:
1. Attraction
2. Engagement
3. Conversion

Attraction metrics group

We get acquainted with the most massive metrics and indicators, impressions, and clicks at the acquisition stage.

An impression is a visual contact between your ad and the visitor. Most sites consider the loading of a page with a banner or ad as an impression, even though we do not know for sure whether a potential client saw the advertising message or not.

The oldest form of payment for online advertising is **pay per thousand clicks** (CPC, Cost per click). Banner ads, video ads, and most media formats are paid for to get impressions then clicks.

A click is when a user clicks on an advertisement. Cost-per-click (CPC) is the second popular form of payment for online advertising. The ratio of clicks to impressions is called **click-through rate or CTR**. For example, an ad has ten clicks with 200 impressions; the CTR will be 5%. Although you will find CTR in all the reports of advertising platforms, it is by no means an estimate of your advertising's effectiveness, and even more so, you should not dwell on CTR statistics.

CTR gives an understanding of 2 important things:
1. the quality of the advertising message
2. targeting accuracy.

Web analytics - how to evaluate the result? | 27

The quality of the advertising message
We can write:

- We are a cool company, so order SEO from us.

Or:

- Webpromo is a Google Premier Partner and has had over 500 successful projects. Order now and receive a 20% discount on an audit!

Which option will be more clickable? Probably the second, but like everything in internet marketing, it's best to test it!

Remember, CTR and engagement are not the end all be all statistics. Your task is to get the user to take action.

Example- Let's say we have two YouTube video ads to get users to register for a free seminar. The first video ad was shown four times less than the second, but the conversion rate was still significantly higher for the first. That means you did something right in the first ad and something wrong in the second ad. Always test different ad formats and messages and measure their effectiveness. I want you to use CTR to get a basic idea of which direction to go.

If you have three ads:
A: CTR 10%,
B: CTR 12%,
C: CTR 3%,

Then, all things being equal, something is wrong with ad C. Either the targeting is inaccurate, or there was a mistake in the ad text, etc. But besides the CTR, it is extremely important to analyze whether these users made a conversion action. We will talk about this later.

Engagement group

At the stage of interactivity, we try to assess how the incoming users are involved in the site's content. To do this, we use metrics such as bounce rate, time spent by a user on a site, and the number of pages viewed per session. Let's take a closer look at the terms I just mentioned.

Bounce rate is the percentage of users who only viewed one page. The user could be on the site for 30 seconds or 30 minutes, but the user left from the same page from which they entered. A high bounce rate could be a warning sign that the site is not engaging the audience well, and, most likely, something is wrong with the site or with the traffic. We need to understand the logic of making a purchase decision. In most niches, users will prefer ordering through a call over ordering using a shopping cart. What does this mean for us in terms of bounce rate? When a person orders through a call, they gain awareness of the product through our website; this won't show up as a conversion on the website. We received an actual order, but the user is displayed in analytics as a refusal. For this reason, I recommend looking at the bounce rate figures as more of a comparative statistic. Compare the bounce rate with similar landing pages and traffic sources to determine if your content is bad or simply how the users interact with content within that specific niche.

Time on the site is also not a straightforward metric. To calculate the time spent on a website, web analytics factor in the time it takes to transition from page to page. Web analytics systems do not count the time spent on the last page.

Example- The user viewed three pages on your site. He spent 2 minutes on the first and second page, but there was an interesting video on the third, and he stayed there for 20 minutes. But, as I stated before, the time on the last page is not counted. And for Vasily and Google Analytics, 4 minutes will be counted instead of the actual 24. I don't want you to overreact to bounce rate numbers and the time spent on your site. A digital marketer must consider each case individually. Perhaps a site has an extremely inconvenient interface, and a user spends a huge amount of time finding what they need.

The number of pages viewed per visit - An obvious metric to measure is how many pages a user views per visit. Everything is clear and transparent here. You should pay attention to how these three indicators compare in traffic sources.

Example using a major news portal

Partners bring about one million traffic per month, and search engines bring in one hundred thousand traffic per month. The average marketer will say that the partners are more important than the search engines, thereby making two mistakes:
1. Always analyze more than one indicator.
2. Focus on qualitative rather than quantitative metrics.

Let's take a look at this same data with the addition of interactivity metrics.

	Traffic / month	% refusals	Time	Viewing depth
Partners	1,000,000	97	0:00:18	1.1
Search engines	100,000	43	0:03:41	3.5

Now it becomes clear that in pursuit of quantity, the project completely forgot about the quality of the audience it attracted. **Important!** Monitor the quality of your competitors' interactivity through Similarweb and continually improve your content and site, as well as the traffic quality of the sources you attract. Now we can get to the most important part, which is determining conversions.

4.3 Conversion group

It is important to understand that actual sales largely depend on how we process requests from a site. To measure and count this entire funnel, we need to find out the conversion rate.

What is a conversion? A conversion is a useful action that a user does on a website. The conversion rate is the percentage of users out of the total audience who perform a useful action. Conversions are divided into two categories: macro conversions and micro conversions (less important). A business wants to calculate understandable and measurable indicators such as calls, orders, and requests. Marketers call these leads, and we classify these as macro conversions. The problem with macro conversions is that there are not a lot of them. The percentage of users who perform macro conversions is from 0.1 to 3%. The conversion rate largely depends on the subject matter, product, site quality, traffic, and many other factors.

To make the right decisions, we need more information about what potential customers are doing on our website. For example, let's say you run 1000 ads. From the above statistics, it's safe to say we would only receive around ten orders. So what do you do now? You need to collect more data. At this moment, micro conversions come to our aid. Micro conversions are user actions on a site that indicate a commercial interest in your product or service.

These include:

- Visiting pages of interest (contacts, promotions, warranty, delivery)
- Downloads (prices, presentations, contracts)
- Subscriptions (social networks, newsletters, etc.)
- Any other actions that express user interest.

Important! If, after reading this chapter, if you choose to simply list your conversions in a table, you would be spending your time wisely. What cannot be measured cannot be improved! The easiest way to improve your digital marketing is through simple conversion tracking.

Marketer's Cheat Sheet - Conversions for Different Projects

1. Online store

Macro conversions:

- Order using a call
- Order using the cart
- Order in one click

Micro conversions:

- Add to cart button
- Online chat
- Contacts page
- Warranty and Delivery page
- Promotions page
- User registration

- User authorization
- Subscription to a newsletter
- Subscription to social networks
- Using site search
- Download price list

2. Service site

Macro conversions:

- Order through a call
- Sending a feedback form

Micro conversions:

- Online chat
- Clients / Portfolio page
- Download the presentation of the company
- Contacts page
- Promotions page
- Subscription to the newsletter
- Subscription to social networks

3. Brand website

Macro conversions:

- Call the hotline
- Sending a feedback form
- Viewing contacts
- Viewing the list of dealers
- Page «Where to buy?»

Micro conversions:

- Download the presentation of the company
- Viewing contacts page
- Subscription to the newsletter
- Subscription to social networks

4. Content project website

Macro conversions:

- Traffic about quality indicators (refusals, viewing depth)
- Subscription to social networks
- Subscription to the newsletter
- Subscription to push notifications

Micro conversions:

- Comments
- Likes, shares
- Participation in a survey
- Viewing a section of a special project
- Using site search

Absolute and Relative Conversions

When starting to work with conversions, it is important to remember two extremely important points:

- Absoluteness and relativity of conversions
- Assisted conversions

Now we will write these complex words in simple language.

Absoluteness and relativity of conversions

Often, when analyzing traffic sources, users look at the conversion rate first. For example, a source with a 7% conversion rate is considered better than another one with 1%. The problem is by focusing on a qualitative indicator; you lose understanding of the **absolute values** (the number of requests, calls) and the cost of attracting them.

Example

Mailing lists conversion rates are several times higher than that of advertising. In our case, it is 15-20 times higher. Simultaneously, it is difficult for us to scale this channel, as the number of unsubscriptions and complaints about spam increases when mailing with commercial information rather than useful content. Advertising, in turn, remains scalable.

Assisted conversion

Customers don't make a purchase decision right away. It usually takes a few «touches» for a user to collect their thoughts and buy something. Imagine dreaming of a new phone. You are thinking about buying it, but the price might be a bit high. One day an ad appears for the phone you wanted, and the price is very reasonable. You immediately click on the ad and immediately start scanning the terms of purchase. The reason for the price change was yesterday a newer model for that phone was announced. All you have to do is click buy, and the phone is yours, but you don't do it. You then go on various price comparison websites, and what do you know, the same online store pops up. This gives you peace of mind because you know that you have done your research and have truly found the best price. But you are still not satisfied. You go to social media looking for even better deals, and you come across the same online store. Now you are almost absolutely convinced that this online store offers the best price. What do I want you to learn from this little scenario? That a price aggregator (like hotline) and a social network platform could become a conversion source. This is called an **assisted conversion**.

I'll take this scenario even further. You still decide not to buy the product, and you decide to see how much money you have. You return to your computer or phone the next day, and you type in «buy iPhone from such and such store» and place an order. The problem is that analytic systems will say that the search engine was the tool that brought you the sale, but it was actually those two associating sources. Only taking into account last-click conversions can screw up your marketing campaign. Sometimes assisted conversion chains are short, and sometimes they are long and complex, as shown in the figure below.

AN ASSISTED CONVERSION is credited to a source involved in the purchase decision but did not directly lead to the final order. Tracking conversions and their value is the minimum that you can start doing right now, and in a couple of months, you will see how your digital marketing is improving. At the very least, this can serve as a better understanding of your audience in terms of conversions! As your analytical tools evolve, you will compare how the distribution of performance differs in the last-click model. For example, in Google Analytics, this data is collected in the Attribution Models report.

Example - Who visits WebPromoExperts more often, men or women? Any analyst will be able to find out that it is 50/50. How about finding out who loves free events more? To find out, set up the «Register for a free event» conversion tracking. What will we see? 75% of the audience are men, and 25% are women. Who ends up buying the courses? Women 65% of the time and men 35% of the time.

ROI (return on investment)

ROI is used to see if funds were spent efficiently. This is calculated in different ways, and you can easily embarrass a marketer during a presentation by asking how he calculated ROI. We will focus on the way Google Analytics interprets ROI.

ROI = (revenue-ad spend) * 100% / ad spend
For example, we spent $ 1000 on Facebook ads and sold for $ 3500
ROI = (3500-1000) * 100% / 1000 = 250%

What does this 250% figure mean? For 1 dollar invested in advertising, we get sales for 2.5. This figure gives an understanding of the effectiveness of the advertising channel.

Example - For an online store, the ROI of PPC advertising is 370% and 1250% for SEO. These figures are your profit.

LTV (Lifetime Value)

LTV is the gross profit that the client brings to you during his or her life cycle. Getting high LTV requires high-quality work with the client base. LTV is a big part of large online stores or businesses operating in global markets.

Example of LTV.

One of our clients writes student papers for money, and most advertising sources have negative ROI. Does this mean that the business is wasting away and dying? No!

An average student places orders on such services at least three times. The first order is usually a trial order for a small amount. They check the quality of the work and whether there is a problem of plagiarism, etc. Next, the student puts an order in for a term paper, and this where the business starts to make money. If a student eventually gets their diploma, you hit the lottery because this gives great PR and LTV to your company! Calculating LTV by channel is important for any business where a customer buys something more than once.

Results by performance indicators
1. Don't pay too much attention to quantitative indicators like impressions, clicks, CTR, likes, followers.
2. Form a list of macro and micro conversions for yourself, record them monthly.
3. In the quarterly and annual periods, try to estimate ROI and LTV indicators for the channels used.

When you start, don't strive for perfection immediately. Start counting conversions, then ROI, then LTV. It is not a fast track, but it will greatly improve your digital marketing.

4.4 Measuring conversions

Conversions are measured with tools such as Google Analytics. Google Analytics allows you to learn more about an audience and track the effectiveness of advertising channels.

Install Google Analytics
To start tracking data using web analytics, enter this link into your browser:
http://analytics.google.com/

There you will find a simple registration process, and you'll get a code that you or your programmers will place on all of your site pages.

For these tools to become a conversion calculator, you need to go through a few mandatory steps:
1) Set up goals and events

2) Set up an e-commerce module (for online stores)

Goals and events in Google Analytics

Let's think back to what we have already learned about conversions. For most businesses, this is more or less a standard list of macro conversions (ordering through the phone and ordering through the site) and micro conversions (view pages «contacts,» «about us,» «shares,» and mailing subscriptions). Using Google Analytics, you can track these conversions and use that data in the future to improve your understanding of your audience and the efficiency of your advertising channels.

If Google Analytics has no targets, it will show you how much traffic each channel is receiving. Even though we would know how much traffic each channel is receiving, we would still be analytically blind since we don't know anything about the data's nuances. For example, in our practice, we analyze conversion rates by age. People ages 18-24 used to order courses 1.5 times more often than that of our primary targeted audience of people ages 25-34. After seeing this data, we shifted our marketing focus to be more involved in student activities in economic and marketing universities, thus boosting our conversion rates.

What do you need to do to get the necessary data into your web analytics account?

You need to understand that there are four types of goals. Two of them are more suitable for commercial projects, and the other two are exclusively for content.

Let's start with the commercial goals first:

1. **The destination URL.** You can record a visit to a landing page by using a «Thank You For Order» page when a visitor submits an application, or you can use micro-conversion pages such as contact, warranty, and delivery pages.

2. **Goal-event.** It will be useful when something important happens on your website, but the landing page URL does not change.

Content projects aim:

3. **The number of pages the user has viewed.**

4. **Time spent on the site**

Let's go through how to set up business goals in Google Analytics. Let's start with something simple like setting goals for the destination

URL. The first thing you need to figure out is how to get the user to navigate to the Thank you URL page so you can measure orders. Suppose it is at site.com/thanks. To set up the target in Google Analytics, we only need to insert «tail»/thanks. If an agency or developer has given you access to an analytics account, you're likely to have limited reporting options.

Set up a landing page in Google Analytics.
Google Analytics has a lot of customizable tools available in the Administrator tab. Administrator/Target/Target/Target. The next step is to specify your «tail» and press the save button! Now in any of the conversion tab reports, you can view data about achieving your goal.

Examples of questions you can answer by setting goals:
1. How many people signed up for my newsletter are from New York?
2. Who uses the callback form more often? Men or women?
3. How many orders do mobile users make?

If you have an online store, I recommend you set up an e-commerce module in Google Analytics. After setting up this module, you will have a thorough understanding of key business indicators such as the amount of an order, the name of the ordered product, and the average price of an order.

What benefits can you get?
How much money each audience segment and advertising channel is bringing you and a better understanding of how a product is ordered.

Source / Medium	Sessions	Ecommerce Conversion Rate	Transactions	Revenue
	32,931	0.05%	18	$5,317.64
1. google / organic	18,034	0.01%	2	$659.34
2. (direct) / (none)	4,571	0.09%	4	$1,804.85
3. google / cpc	1,530	0.07%	1	$28.86
4. sendpulse / email	1,528	0.07%	1	$17.99
5. facebook / cpc	1,459	0.14%	2	$554.62

Tracking calls
Last but not least is the importance of understanding call tracking. A lot of people are going to call asking for information about your

product. But how will you know where this person is calling from. Is he calling from New York? California maybe? What about how he even found you in the first place? Did he or she visit your website and decide to call and order something? When people talk about how they found out about a product, they typically say:

- From the Internet
- From friends
- The site itself

There are three principles of call tracking:
1. Hiding contact information
2. Use promo codes
3. Actual call tracking

Let's take a closer look at each of these principles.

Hiding contact information

This method is the cheapest out of all the possible options. You need to discuss with your programmer how to get the user to click on your contacts link so you can log that information into your database.

Use promo codes

This method is already less associated with web analytics and more with your CRM system (process of measuring order sources). Whatever a user interacts with; whether it be with a mailing, banner, or a promotion on a social network, the user should receive a promo code. When activated, this promo code should give the user some type of bonus, discount, or gift.

Call tracking system

A call tracking system will allow you to clearly see which channels are effective. Call-tracking can be divided into three different categories: classic, dynamic, and promo codes. Use one number per source.

Dynamic call-tracking

Why is dynamic call tracking such a game changer? Because it allows you to see who is online at an exact moment.

Call-tracking by promo codes
Combines promo codes and call-tracking, making it much more affordable.

The history of one restaurant
Strengths of call tracking tool:

- Understanding the effectiveness of marketing activities
- customer service information.

One of our restraint clients had terrible customer service. This is a common theme among businesses. You can have a cool site that brings in a lot of traffic, but the person picking up the phone on your side can kill the customer's desire to work with you in less than a minute. Now we understand conversions, but the puzzle is still unfinished. There is still ambiguity when it comes to where the user is from.

		Acquisition		
Source / Medium		Users	New Users	Sessions
		1,838	1,411	2,393
		% of Total	% of Total	% of Total
		7.91% (23,227)	7.59% (13,085)	7.27% (32,931)
1.	facebook / cpc	1,234 (66.02%)	1,022 (72.43%)	1,459 (60.97%)
2.	facebook / post	216 (11.56%)	119 (8.43%)	350 (14.63%)
3.	m.facebook.com / referral	151 (8.08%)	123 (8.72%)	165 (6.90%)
4.	l.facebook.com / referral	118 (6.31%)	45 (3.19%)	221 (9.24%)
5.	facebook / event	90 (4.82%)	69 (4.89%)	120 (5.01%)

URL builder
Along with understanding targeted actions, it is important to know where the visitor came from. To answer this question, you need to get acquainted with **a URL builder.** One of the most important things that web analytics systems give us is the segmentation of traffic sources. The campaign, the ad, and the advertising request can help us determine where the user who performed the desired action on the site came from. This is not the default. For example, going into the traffic source report in Google Analytics, you'll find a Facebook/referral bar responsible for showing you all the traffic from this social network. A URL

layout tool and Facebook Advertising complement each other because it helps Google Analytics determine where your traffic is coming from.

Like any other company, in 2010, we launched a business page and a paid advertising campaign. Our instructions to our employees were simple: «Go to every social network, like everything, then comment and repost content.» After a while, the Facebook/referral bar generated a substantial amount of growth within our business, but there came a time when there were applications for SEO and PPC advertising. Then the question arose which channels are generating the most leads? We were able to find out after we went to the URL builder and agreed that we tag all links. The result was quite interesting. The company's Facebook page generated the most traffic, but it did not generate leads. As we later realized, the content was too complicated for the client audience. I then worked extremely hard to get myself acquainted with everyone in the digital marketing field by regularly speaking at events and handing out business cards.

The URL builder tool has become an integral part of understanding our audience, and it has also helped our mailing, banner, social network, and PPC advertising. It is of the utmost importance to use a URL builder for any internet promotion tool in which you invest time or money.

Once I go through the following instructions, I recommend closing this book and doing some practice. Using the URL builder tool, let's show Google Analytics properly recognize your traffic sources.

Enter the URL in Google, and let's get to work. Start with the landing page first. This is where you lure the audience in. Your landing page can be a product page, a category page, or an article on a blog.

You must follow three parameters to be successful:

Source - A website or a partner on which a link is placed.
Channel - Your website or partner website that brings you traffic. These could be mailing lists, paid advertising, articles, social media, and messenger groups.
Campaign - What exactly are we advertising?

Do you doubt whether you need it?
I will give a simple example from our practice. Everyone loves social media. Marketers and business owners often believe that everything you do on the internet should start with social media. According

to our analytics, we have about 60 active groups on Facebook with an audience of more than 1000 people. When we posted an announcement, how many of these groups do you think generated traffic? Three!

Now let's think about this from a practical point of view. How long do you think it would take for a content manager to post all these links? Probably at least two hours. We just saved two hours of time and resources by using a URL builder. A URL builder and correct web analytics are things that most people know about, but they tend not to use them. My advice is to add these tools to your digital marketing campaign so you can better understand what is going on with your company online.

What should be done after all of this?
1. Take the time to set goals and events.
2. Set aside a couple of hours for programmers to set up an e-commerce module if you have an online store
3. Determine how you plan to count calls.

4.5 Web Analytics Tools to Improve the Site

One of the most valuable web analytics system applications is to work to increase the conversion rate on a site. We have already learned how to measure conversions. Now it's time to increase them.

Google Analytics has a separate service that allows you to improve conversion rates using A/B testing campaigns. You can launch several different campaigns at one time and see which one is the most effective. That way, you can make an informed decision on which campaign is best and you can avoid guessing.

What does Google Analytics do?
Google Analytics allows you to download up to 6 different versions of a page and set a traffic condition.

When you're experimenting, it's critical to understand the main conversion and what you will measure. You'll need:

- A Programmer
- A Designer
- A project manager or marketer who will oversee the campaign

Example - We worked with an online store that sells generators. We wanted to experiment on the pages of the product categories. By changing the layout, we were able to increase their conversions by 3.5 times. The online store had 3.5 times more orders with the same volume of traffic.

Conclusions and recommendations

Web analytics is the pulse of any online business. If you take analytics seriously, you can measure anything and everything.

This is a really simple checklist that you can use:
1. Review your list of business goals that you made during the first chapter
2. Make a list of macro and micro-conversions for your business.
3. Start to measure it in Google Analytics.
4. Experiment, analyze, then optimize your marketing campaigns!

For me, analytics has become my favorite part of digital marketing, and now that you understand them, you will love them too.

4.6 Web analytics checklist

When you finish this chapter, you will have a cheat sheet that will help your business take advantage of digital marketing's most important thing: measurability.

1. Form the SMART goals for your business and online project.
S – Specific
M – Measurable
A – Achievable
R - Relevant
T – Time-bound
Example- Get $10,000 in net profit in the second quarter of this year

2. Write down your macro and micro conversions (You can use your marketing cheat sheet from this chapter)

An example of an academy
Macro conversions:

Ordering a course through a form
Ordering a course through a call
Micro conversion:
Subscription
Registration for a free event
Subscription to social media profiles

3. Implement the above macro and micro conversions in the Google Analytics settings and call tracking systems.
You need to set up:

- Goals and events
- An E-commerce module for your online store
- Determine what approach you will take to track calls

An example from WebPromoExperts

Source / Medium	Sessions	Ecommerce Conversion Rate	Transactions	Revenue
	32,931	0.05%	18	$5,317.64
1. google / organic	18,034	0.01%	2	$659.34
2. (direct) / (none)	4,571	0.09%	4	$1,804.85
3. google / cpc	1,530	0.07%	1	$28.86
4. sendpulse / email	1,528	0.07%	1	$17.99
5. facebook / cpc	1,459	0.14%	2	$554.62

4. Start tagging all the links through the URL layout to clearly understand from which sources key request applications and orders are coming.

5. Regularly check your KPI's once a month, once in a quarter, once a year.

Chapter 5
Portrait of the target audience. Forming a user persona

5.1 Who is your client?
5.2 Audience data from web analytics systems
5.3 Audience data from social media pages statistics
5.4 Audience polls

- Who is your client?
- What do your web analytic systems know about your client?
- What do your social network channels know about your client?
- What information have you gathered from your offline marketing (survey, questionnaire, interviews)?

5.1 Who is your client?

The portrait of a target audience answers the question of who your client is. The avatar is the ideal potential client you want to attract. When clients come to our agency, the first question we ask them is, «Who needs your product or service?». The answer is usually «Everyone», in other words, this an unclear and unspecific portrait and is one reason why they are probably not having success with their marketing.

To form a user persona, you need the following data:

- Gender
- Age
- Interests
- Location
- Language
- Income level
- Education
- The average amount of money they spend

- What they want from your product
- Fears about your product
- What their primary needs are
- How familiar they are with your product (from 1-10)
- How the client interacts with an offline product
- How the clients interact online with you

Where can we get this data from?
1. Web Analytics Systems (Google Analytics)
2. Data from the statistics of social media pages like Facebook, YouTube, Instagram, etc.
3. Advertising planners and Facebook Audience Insights.
4. Audience surveys via mailing lists
5. Doing interviews with 10-20 real customers who are willing to buy your product

5.2 Audience data from web analytics systems

Google Analytics can tell us the following things about the visitors who come to our site :

- Gender and age
- Interests
- Location
- Devices they use and browsers they use
- Keywords
- Most visited pages, products, and services.

The most useful data can be found in the Audience Tab. I recommend that you thoroughly examine this tab. If you're already tracking conversions, look at the traffic section's data and the conversion section. If you look at our analytics by gender and age, it becomes clear that for us, you need to form at least two avatars. Men ages 25-34 and women ages 25-34. Later we added a younger avatar 18-24 (student) and an older avatar (35-44 entrepreneur).

5.3 Audience data from social media pages statistics

If you have a social media page that doesn't have many subscribers, you can apply the same methodology. Now I will go into detail about the main features.

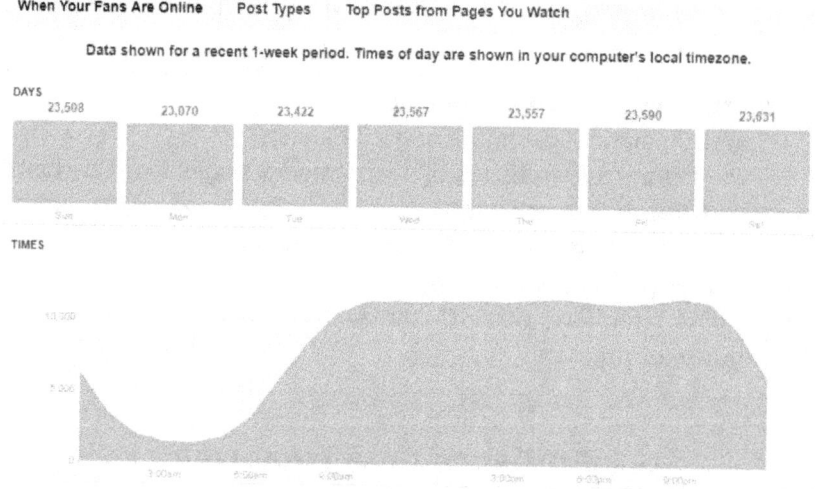

The statistics of Facebook pages are among the most exciting information that you can learn because it gives you an understanding of how your content is consumed.

The statistics of Instagram pages are very similar to what Facebook and other social networks give, such as gender, age, and location.

YouTube statistics give an exciting opportunity to analyze the video preferences of an exact video.

Facebook Audience Insights or Audience Statistics is a tool for evaluating audiences on Facebook.

You will receive the following information:

- Gender
- Age
- Interests
- Marital status
- Education level
- The post
- Location
- Languages
- Devices

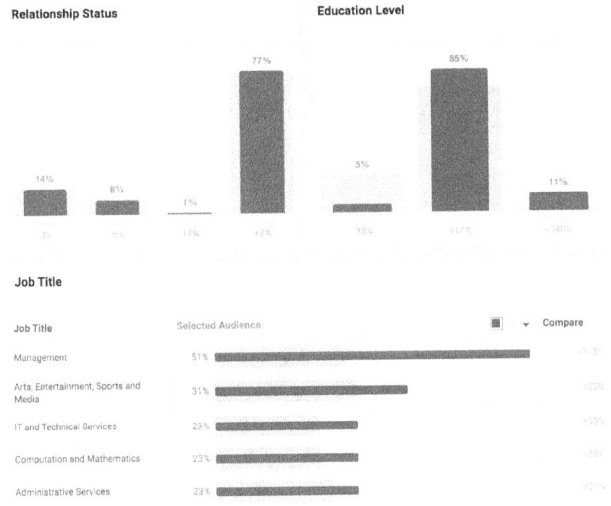

For businesses operating in the U.S. market, the following information will be of interest to you:

- Family income
- Homeowner or tenant
- How they spend their money
- Online shopping behaviors
- Purchasing behaviors

5.4 Audience polls

You can meet your audience's expectations by sending them surveys in mailings. It is always good to offer them some kind of bonus or discount for completing a survey. Here are some questions that we asked our students:

- How would you describe the WebPromoExperts Academy to your friend?
- What problem did you want to solve when you were training with us?
- Describe how WebPromoExperts helped solve the problem?
- What were the results of training with us?
- How has your project and your life changed since then?
- Write the three most important reasons that convinced you to enroll in our course?
- What can we do better?

What's next?

You have your data from your analytics, social networks, and survey forms. Now It's time to draw the portraits.

Andrew, **entrepreneur** 42 years old

Owner of a small company specializing in car service. He realized that the internet is necessary to build his business, so he hired an Internet marketer, but he eventually wants to do all the marketing himself. His income is above average. As of right now, he spends little time on the internet. He does a fundamental analysis of his competitors, and he orders spare parts for his business online. He values his time and useful information. He considers free webinars to be valuable content, and he is interested in articles like «How to become an Internet marketer.»

Hanna, **marketer**, 29 years

A marketer who works as a project manager for an online store. She's an active Facebook user, and she's subscribed to multiple professional business resources. Hanna is interested in traveling, buying clothes, and watching movies. She is ambitious, organized, and values her time.

Max, **Internet Marketer,** 32 years old

Max is a young internet marketing specialist. He has a sales company that sells metal and plastic windows. His income level is average. His company cannot afford the agency's services yet, so Max does all the marketing himself. He signed up for the WebPromoExperts newsletter, and he attends as many free events as possible. He has passed his first internet marketing course and wants to learn more. He is into cars, and he is a family man. On the internet, he uses professional resources to monitor his competitors' websites, and in his spare time, he likes to learn about new gadgets, watch movies, and learn life hacks that can help him around the house. He is looking for a solution to problems that he is having, and he becomes irritated if he does not find them. Max is a curious person. He reads a lot of business and personal development information. Max has many questions regarding our case studies, and I would be glad to give this information to him for free. A user persona can paint a picture of what the consumer wants and helps you avoid the problem of putting your wants and interest in front of theirs. Once you have created your user personas, you can move on to the next step. Let's take a look at WebPomoExperts academy's mission; «help businesses increase online sales.» Free webinars can help give basic ideas to new entrepreneurs on how to go about marketing online.

Chapter 6
Content

6.1 Using blogs
6.2 Video content
6.3 Event Content
6.4 Who's responsible for everything?

Content is the core of digital marketing. Start creating content only after you have completed the steps in the previous sections. Content marketing starts with planning. You should have a clear goal in mind and have an idea of how you will write your articles, shoot your videos, and hold events. The first stage is to determine your reach. Your reach is how many views an article or video has and how much traffic it has brought to your site's pages. The second stage is about measuring community growth. Measuring community growth is done by counting the number of subscribers in your mailing lists and the followers on your social networks (Facebook, YouTube, etc.).The third and most crucial stage is to link your community growth to your conversions. To simplify this task, it makes sense to calculate the number of buy requests from each of these four channels:

- Direct traffic (brand recognition)
- Social media
- Organic search
- Email traffic

For example, this was the increase in order requests for WebpromoExperts last year:

- Direct traffic: 135%
- Social media: 236%
- Organic search 131%
- Mailings: 65%

A content plan is a table that tells us what was responsible for the growth within our company. It could be the videos you created, the events you held, etc. The data you receive reflects what the audience deems most important. Was it your articles or webinars? Maybe it was your YouTube videos or online broadcasts? To form a quality project plan, you need to describe in full detail the following things:
1. Who your audience is
2. Which content is preferred
3. What the best time to post is
4. Which format is best
5. The number of people you want to reach
6. Decide to use paid or free content

6.1 Using blogs

Next, you need to decide which format to use. The most common form of content marketing is blog posting. Blog posting combines the most popular types of content formats, and it allows content to be distributed efficiently. One thing people typically get confused with is the difference between a blog and a news story? A company news strategy is saying I'm sexy, and I know it. We are writing about what is interesting for us and not our audience. Most companies write news articles twice a year, and the rest of the time, the site is never updated. Make sure that you do not do this.

A blog is a vibrant community that responds to the needs and problems of your audience. The most common formats of blog posts are the answers to specific **questions.** We have already talked about the Serpstat service. Using Serpstat will help you find the questions your Google Audience has, and you can use this information for your content marketing. Although blogging is a very effective way to market content, it's quite challenging to implement. Even for us, it wasn't easy to get our employees to write blogs. We ended up circumventing this problem by using short YouTube marketing clips (2-5 minutes). Our employees found it much easier to talk about our content rather than to write about it.

Needs will appear across all niches. Having strong expert content will help grow an audience on your blog. Content can be **interviews** with people who are experts in your field. I am sure there will be a large number of resources in your niche that you will collect and use to promote such interviews. Peer-reviewed research and surveys are excellent content for your audience. I have a newsletter and social network audience that I communicate with regularly to gauge their interest in specific topics. You can conduct your mini-research by interviewing your audience about what they are interested in and then generate content for them based on what you find out.

Ratings.
People love ratings because it tells us who's right and who's not.

Press and post-releases.
PR announcements and post releases should be used to update the audience on what's going on with your company.

Behind the scenes content
There should be information about a product on a blog as well. Include behind-the-scenes details like what you've added and removed to make the product better. Ensure the details about your product are short and simple because we don't want to bore our readers. Your primary content will consist of blogging, and it will be the main force that drives your content marketing in the right direction, so you need to develop a blog first.

6.2 Video content

This is the format that is tearing up all the indicators right now. These are generally videos on YouTube. Video content should be either useful or interesting. The video doesn't have to be of the highest quality but make sure your videos don't look like they're shot on a flip phone, and the audio is decent. This will be enough to collect subscribers and grow your YouTube channel.

You must integrate your video content into the rest of your activities. While making video content, create subtitles and use this text as blog content on your site. The best video formats for blogs are Q&As, reviews, news, interviews, tutorials, and short digests. An essential thing in a YouTube video is personality. In my experience, many businesses pay attention to the quality of the video first, but I'm afraid that's not right. YouTube is about the quality of content, not the picture in the background. Realizing this fact will make it much easier for you to start making videos.

Look at the columns below to see what kinds of videos we produced:

- **Internet marketing hacks** -quick tips on using tools, services, and process optimization.
- **Q&A** - answers to questions of the audience.
- **Meeting with an expert is a** type of interview format
- **Digital Marketing Cases** - Stories about the successes and failures of other projects

6.3 Event Content

The format of event content is associated with the B2B segment. Event content is when you use offline seminars, webinars and online broadcasts to present your new product or service in a wide range of niches.

Types of events
Events are divided into two categories:

- Face-to-face (offline) - conferences, seminars, workshops, individual training.
- Remote (online) - webinars, online broadcasts, online presentations, live meetings.

It is easy to measure and understand the effectiveness of event content. When you start choosing formats, you need to understand your goals. A conference is one of the most expensive formats, but at the same time, it can increase brand recognition and loyalty. You might have to prepare six months in advance and gather speakers, but it'll be worth it in the end. A smaller event is a workshop. It can be half a day or a full day. A seminar format is a tool that is best suited for regularly feeding the customer base information and attracting new, potential, loyal customers.

The most potent online event is a webinar. The webinar is a small meeting that only lasts for a couple of hours. The webinar format allows you to reach a vast audience. Offline events are designed for people in your city, but online webinars can help you reach markets worldwide.

Webinars can help you have a customer base with which you can communicate with through emails. The event-content format is one of the most progressive ways to solve business problems like attracting new customers, increasing loyalty from existing customers, and increasing brand recognition.

6.4 Who's responsible for everything?

How should content marketing be organized? What is a digital marketer? If you start creating content, you have to have a strategist. A strategist is someone who makes decisions and understands what we're doing and why and knows the answers to the questions we asked at the beginning of this book. He must clearly understand the target audience and what goals the company should achieve.

For small companies, the owner is more than likely to act as the strategist. For larger companies, it will be a mix between the owner and a marketer. A medium-size business has a CMO (Chief Marketing Officer) that acts as its strategist. You must have a good strategist within your company because if you look outside your company for a strategist, you'll run into some problems. An outsider will never 100% understand your company or your product. In small companies, a marketer can write the text for your content. So if you have employed the correct people, the quality of the content will be high, which is one of the advantages of having a smaller company.

All graphic content is based on the designer. This is the person who will select all of your images, retouch them if they need retouching, and they are also responsible for creating your thumbnails. The cameraman and video editor can be a single person. Although if you have the budget, you can form a whole team to make your video content. If you regularly do events, hold webinars, conferences, and seminars, you should have an administrator that oversees these things. It just makes everything a lot easier and more organized.

Once you have mastered creating content, you can now move to the distribution stage. Here we will talk about the importance of promoting your products on search engines (SEO).

Chapter 7
SEO
(Search engine optimization)

7.1 SEO or paid advertising?
7.2 On-Page SEO
7.3 Link building and other factors
7.4 Conclusions, cases, and recommendations
7.5 SEO Checklist

7.1 SEO or paid advertising?

Search engines have become a universal advisor and assistant to today's internet users. We come to Google to find out things like:

- What is the weather like?
- Who are the Lakers playing tonight?
- What time is it in London?

And much more!

But the most important thing for businesses is that the search engine has become quite the advisor in commercial matters like:

- Where to buy something?
- Which model is better to choose?
- Who has the lowest price?
- Is such and such company trustworthy?

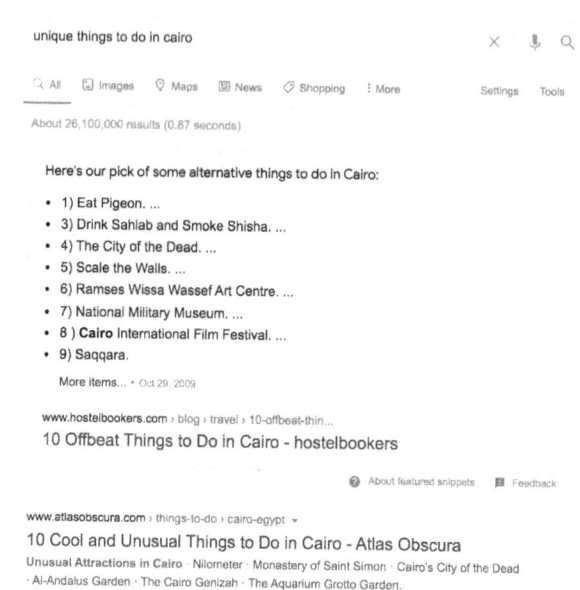

Every day, Google receives 10 billion requests, and the commercial interest of a company is a big part of this 10 billion.

SEO is poorly predicted and targeted. This tool requires a long wait process to achieve results. So If it's that bad, why don't I advise you to skip this chapter altogether? Because despite all of its flaws, SEO has enormous amounts of targeted traffic, and its price is usually many times lower than that of PPC. The next thing we should figure out is how to make sure your company pops up first in search engines.

Google takes into account more than 200 indicators when ranking a site. The most useless and time-consuming thing I could advise you to do right now is to count them.

I've been talking about SEO at seminars and lectures for years. Due to my vast experience on this, I neatly organized all of these indicators into a simple pyramid diagram. Our students and my colleagues used it so much that they started calling it the Voroniuk Pyramid.

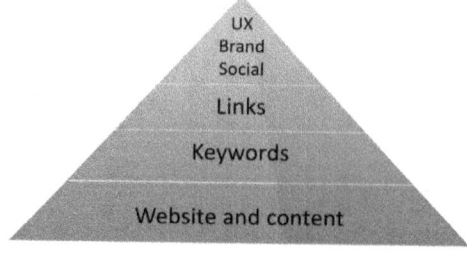

The pyramid is separated into stages. The first and most basic thing that SEO starts with is the website and content. The second stage is keywords. Keywords will determine if users find you by search requests. Find the most suitable keywords for your product and tailor your website around these keywords. The third stage is links. Links are like user voices. Cool content means shared content. The more famous you are on the internet, the more shares you will collect in the form of external links. The total amount of links used to be a factor in determining your position in search engines. The fourth stage is brand recognition within social media. When people write your brand name on the internet, your company is in a good place.

7.2 On-Page SEO

Traffic from search engines has many nuances that require constant interaction with developers. Technical issues can be very tricky.

On-Page SEO consists of a wide range of tasks such as:

- Setting up server responses and redirecting them.
- Opening and banning individual site pages on search engines
- Creating maps of a site (sitemap.xml)
- Improving the visibility of site descriptions in search engines
- Properly forming page addresses
- Working with the internal links of a site
- And more

Since most of these things require our reader to be reasonably technically trained, we will elaborate on some of the most important criteria:

- Availability
- Download speed
- Availability in search engines.

Availability

Any long-term problems can lead to the loss of traffic and customers. Now that we know the importance of site availability, let's look at this technical setup of a server response, and let's also examine a few fundamental search optimization time rules. You can find out the response of your website's page server with a third-party service. By default, if the page is available for both bots and humans, the server response is «200 OK.»

If the page is not found/does not exist, the answer is «404 Not Found.» I'm sure that you have run into these error messages before.

The second important rule **is, NOT to change the URLs if you can avoid it.** Search engines are sensitive to URL changes. If a change to an address is unavoidable, have your programmers install a 301 to redirect your audience from the old page to the new one. The same goes for a domain change. Try to avoid changing the domain, if possible.

Download speed and mobility

Download speed and mobility are critical in today's digital landscape and are becoming increasingly important because of increased shared mobile traffic.

The download speed should be 1-3 seconds, and you will need the following tools to ensure that you are on the right track.

Pingdom Tools - Gives a download speed figure. The information will be evident not only to developers but also to the average internet user. The download speed affects the ranking of your site. If your site loads at a rate of about 4 seconds (3 recommended), and most competitors are more than 5 seconds, you will win in this category, and your ranking on search engines will be better. Your website's position will depend on how well you can follow the requirements in this chapter.

Google Page Speed Insights - shows the speed of your website. Google Page speed insights will help your developer improve your website's speed.

Google Mobile-Friendly Test Tool - Yes/no, to the question: «Is my site friendly if the user comes to it from a mobile device?»

SEO (Search engine optimization)

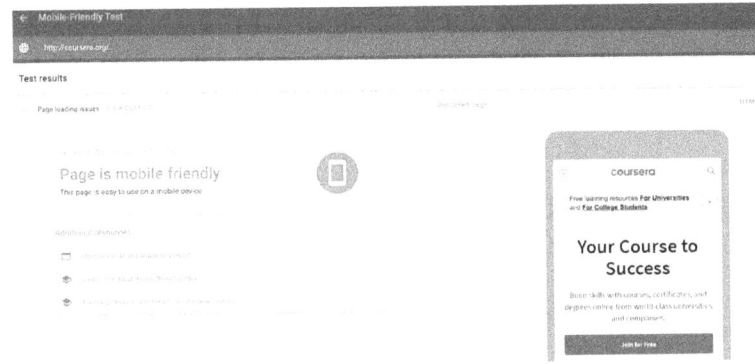

Presence in search engines

By entering the site: mysite.com into Google, you can find out what Google sees. These figures are like a trip to the doctor. If your doctor looks at you and says you're sick, it's probably a good idea to let him examine you. When your site is not looking good, and you see that the number of pages is 0, there is a problem.

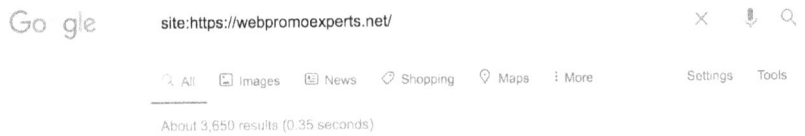

The next step is to identify the problem areas of your search engine optimization and to register the tools for Google Search Console.

By seeing what you need from Google's Search Console, you can find the answers to the following questions:

- What are the current errors on the site?
- What content is being duplicated?
- Is the site under search engine sanctions?

Now that we have covered SEO audits let's move onto the criteria for text content.

Text content should be:

- At least 500 words
- It must be Unique
- Relevant
- Updated regularly

The user should want to share and use your content. We will talk about this later on as it will play a key role in our strategy. Now let's talk about how to form text correctly.

Text content should be the basis of your website content

Search engines are determining the position of your website by the text on your website. My agency was helping a wedding website draw more traffic to itself. We noticed that they had many beautiful pictures, and all they needed was text content to improve their position in search engines.

The text should be useful

The number of keywords used to be essential but not anymore. How useful the text is to a user is now more important.

The text should be unique

This is the most essential and critical part of content creation.

How to check if there are duplicates of your site?

The easiest way is to copy the text sentence from the page in quotes and paste it using double quotes in a search bar. It is important to check more than one page of a site for duplicates. You can check the category, subcategory, product card, blog article, etc. You can learn a lot of vital information by clicking on the link «Show hidden results.» In addition to this manual check, you can turn to various services and programs to show the percentage of uniqueness. Remember that none of these services will offer you 100% accurate information. There is always the possibility that some duplicates, both internal and external, will not be found. The reasons for the internal duplicate are often either a lack of understanding by the developers of the basics of SEO or the same lack of knowledge of these basics on your part. If a CEO says that three paragraphs should say something like «we are the best of the best company on the market» on all pages, you will have duplicates of text in search engines. When I am giving lectures, I am often asked what to do with the product pages. Descriptions are extremely difficult to make unique. There is a solution, though, and it lies in generating reviews and encouraging users to leave reviews.

SEO (Search engine optimization) | 61

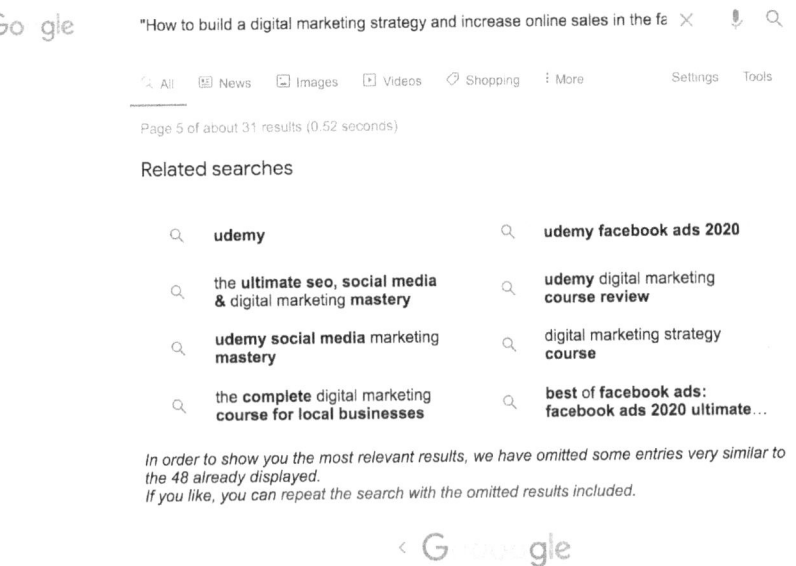

There are usually two reasons for external duplicates. You borrowed texts from someone, and someone borrowed them from you.

What if competitors, in a rush to stay relevant in search engines, stole your text and posted it. Are there any tools to protect yourself from this?

Let's start with the bad news. There is no such thing as a 100% protection guarantee tool, but the tools below reduce the probability that you will be lower in the search results when people steal content from you.

1. Block copying the text on your site. Blocking copying on your site can somewhat prohibit competitors from stealing text from your site.

2. Give a pop-up warning. For resources where it is entirely impossible to block copying, such as news sites, we use a pop-up with a warning.

3. Add a link when smbd copying your content automatically. People are not the only ones who will steal your content; bots will too. By using this tool, you can make bots spread your links and work for you.

4. Write DMCA complaints to Google. If you see someone routinely stealing your content, write a complaint to Google.

Again, it is the text's uniqueness that is one of the most important criteria for ranking your site in search engines. Yes, you will have people who will always try to steal your content, but at least the content will appear on your site first.

Trying to deceive a search engine can lead to severe consequences and lead to your website falling down the search results ranks.

The text should be relevant.

The content of the text should correspond to the keywords that brought the user to the site.

Content should be updated regularly

The more often you add new unique information to a site, the more often a Google Bot will visit your website.

- Do you want to know the last time a bot kept your site in its index? Use the command cache:mysite.com

This is Google's cache of https://web-promo.ua/. It is a snapshot of the page as it appeared on 9 Mar 2021 18:49:53 GMT. The current page could have changed in the meantime. Learn more.
Full version   Text-only version   View source
Tip: To quickly find your search term on this page, press Ctrl+F or ⌘-F (Mac) and use the find bar.

webpromo   Маркетологи за результат!   Контекстная реклама   SEO-продвижение   Повышение конверсии

Keywords. How do you get found?

Keywords are the primary tool that will help target users find you in search results. Two main components go into choosing the right keywords. The first is to choose keywords relevant to your site, and the second is to place them correctly in the website code.

Search for keywords

Keyword selection can consist of several steps:

- Brainstorming
- Using evidence from Google Analytics and Google Search Console
- Using the evidence of competitors from SEMRush, Similarweb, and Serpstat.

SEO (Search engine optimization) | 63

- Use search engine estimates from Google Ads Keyword Planner.

Brainstorming is useful in small teams of 3-5 people. When brainstorming, it's essential to answer the following questions:

- What do we sell? (site structure)
- What are the important parameters in making a decision? (filters and sorting)

For example, an online store that sells home appliances needs to figure out how to get a user from its homepage to the page of the product he wants to buy. The way for a user to navigate to the BOSCH KGV39VW31 refrigerator should look like this:

Home (Home appliances) → Large home appliances → Refrigerators → BOSCH refrigerator (Brand) → BOSCH KGV39VW31 refrigerator

Utilize your keywords on your website and place them in places that will help you succeed. Use commercial buy keywords like the ones below on the left and right-hand side of your page to steer the user towards a purchase.

- Buy Berlin appliances
- Buy large Berlin appliances
- Buy a Berlin fridge
- Buy a BOSCH Berlin refrigerator
- Buy a BOSCH KGV39VW31 refrigerator

A well-defined structure of categories, subcategories, and products will allow a user to navigate your page easier and increase conversions. It is essential to ask what else interests our customers. These parameters will act as a kind of filter when selecting keywords. For example, if you have touristic companies, the structure should something like the following:

Home (Tours)→Tours to Turkey→Tours to Antalya→ Tours in Side → Waterworld Tours

And here are some questions that may still interest our potential tourists:

- How much? (burning tours, price tours, tour cost)
- Where is it? (tours from ...)
- What type of holiday is it? (beach, skiing, sightseeing, etc.)
- Who are we going to vacation with? (with children, groups, etc.)

Keywords are picked up and distributed across the pages of a site. Now the most exciting part is below.

Where to enter keywords on a site to increase the likelihood of getting to the top of the search results:

- Title (meta title)
- The text of the page
- URL
- Internal links
- Description (meta description)

Title

One of the most important elements of On-Page SEO is the title. I recommend that the title length not exceed 65 characters. The title is the thing that will stand out the most, and it should give the visitor a very clear and concise description of the page.

Long ago, people that used SEOs followed the principle of text spam. Text spam is when you repeatedly place the same keywords throughout your site to improve your standing in search engines. The algorithms have changed dramatically, and this is no longer a good way of bettering your position in search engines. That being said, people continue to ask me how many times they should mention a keyword in their text at my seminars. My philosophy is that one time is enough.

URL- How not to do it:
Incorrect: site.com/?id105000
Incorrect: site.com/category100/product500
Incorrect: site.com/ rubble
Correct: site.com/sheben

Entering the URL of a keyword is a positive ranking factor for a search engine. But it's important not to overdo it.

Internal links
Use keywords to refer to other pages of a site.

Description (meta-tag description)
You won't find this item on your pages, but it can be easily found if you open the site code. When we talk about large projects with more than 1000 pages, automatic meta-tag generation of a title and its description is used based on your product database. This generation requires the SEO and the developer to work together closely.

Let's use an online electronics store as an example. Consider the automatic generation of meta tags for phone brands such as Apple, Samsung, Lenovo, etc. What data do we have in the product database? We have the Brand, the number of models, price, availability, and the discount size.

How are meta tags generated?
Headline: Smartphones [Brand]. Buy from [store name] online store. Price, characteristics, reviews.
Description: Mobile phones and smartphones [Brand]. More than [number of offers] models from [min price]. [Current promotion]
How will it work for the Samsung brand?
Title: Samsung smartphones. Buy from the MoiSite online store. Price, characteristics, reviews.
Description: Samsung mobile phones and smartphones. More than 75 models from 200$. Bluetooth headset for free!

On-page SEO in the form of an SEO-audit in the content strategy is mandatory for obtaining search engine optimization results.

7.3 Link building and other factors

As we said earlier, good content is the key to success. It directly affects whether people will talk about you online and whether they will post links to your sites.

Content-marketing is one of the few really white knights and legal opportunities to get the links that search engines consider natural. How do you get links to your site?

Let's go over the good ways and bad ways to get links.

White Hat SEO Link building

1. Content marketing. Create quality content and make sure it stands out.

2. PR activity on the internet. Do journalists and bloggers write about you in online media? Ask journalists to not only mention your company but put a link to your site.

3. Outreach. Create quality content according to the editorial requirements of a popular external site. Specify at the very beginning that, in return for your content, the article will have a direct link to your site. For example, I wrote the article «Top 10 YouTube channels for Digital marketing» for our blog, but at the last moment I decided to give it to the famous publication «Internet News Agency.» By doing this, I acquired 500 new subscribers for my YouTube channel and got a link from a reputable news agency.

4. Working with communities. Encourage communities and forums to ask about your service or product. Here I have to draw the line and say that the following methods of obtaining references are not squeaky clean but fall into a grey area.

Grey SEO

5. Purchase links from webmasters directly. Find popular sites on your subject and agree with the owner about posting an article or newsletter with a link to your content.

6. Purchase links on permanent link exchanges.

Black Hat SEO methodologies:
7. Purchase links on temporary link exchanges.
8. Posting links through link aggregators.

Black (this is not good!):
All kinds of search spam, hacking sites, etc.

I will not deny that the search engine optimization market still mostly operates based on buying links, although their role has dropped significantly in recent years. You have to determine what's best for your company. You can do it the fast way and possibly get into a bit of trouble, or you can do it the natural way and have minimal risks.

Let's discuss what factors search engines take into account in the links that lead to your site. The largest factors are quantitative, qualitative, anchor parameters, and the dynamics of a reference mass's build-up.

To look at this information both on your website and your competitors' sites, I recommend using such services as Ahrefs or Majestic. When analyzing the information on any **number of links**, you need to pay attention to two things. How many external links lead to your site, and how many domains have links to your site.

Analyzing the quality of links is not so simple. The search engine takes into account a vast number of factors.

- The credibility of the domain (the quality of references leading to it);
- Regionality (site region compliance and sources link)
- Type (the proximity of resource themes)

An anchor or text link is called text content when the link leads to your site. SEO's have always tried to manipulate anchors, and as a result, you get something unnatural like this: «buy a laptop,» etc.

You can also analyze the text of anchors through Ahrefs, Majestic, and other similar services. Anchor text still plays a significant role in ranking sites because it creates an incentive to be manipulated. In 2004, the search request for «miserable failure» led people to the biography of George W. Bush on the White House website. Google then edited the algorithm, but some holes remained within the search engine.

To avoid sanctions from search engines, most of the links to your site should refer to you as a brand, but if there are no commercial words describing your activities, your path to the top position of the search engine can be infinitely long.

Search engines have given links a leading role in ranking for so long that there have been times when SEO has worked as an auction. Those who spent a considerable amount on buying links were in higher positions. Those times ended at Google in 2012 with the Google Penguin update.

Sanctions for the manipulation of links.

Google actively penalizes people for trying to cheat different link parameters. This is especially true of aggressive link purchases. Sanctions from search engines can be imposed manually or automatically.

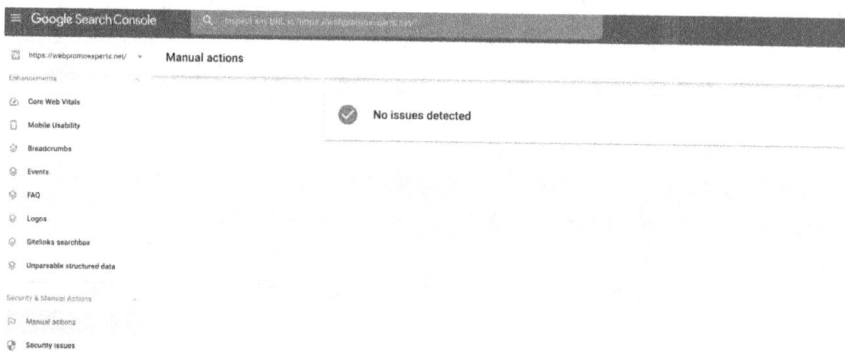

Most manual sanctions can be identified through the Google Search Console. The sanctions can be seen there and within the mail of the owners of the site. We often sarcastically refer to these as «letters of happiness». You can expect a substantial drop-off in search traffic if you get one of these letters.

Automatic sanctions are more complicated. There's a need to track the drop in traffic and superimpose it on the search engine update calendar, which they usually post on their official blogs.

The process of getting out of sanctions is quite long and can take several months. The algorithm is as follows:

- Analyze all links (unload from Ahrefs, Majestic, Google Search Console)
- Appealing to site owners removes the links with the least quality
- The links that couldn't be removed from the text file and downloaded by Google Disavow Tool
- Send a request to recapitulate the site through Google Search Console

Dealing with the lifting of sanctions is the most unpleasant part of search optimization. The ideal situation is not to let this happen.

Other ranking factors

Since 2010, search engines have not only been looking for tools to punish link manipulation but have also done their best to reduce their role overall. Google has focused on building a brand and has begun to consider two factors: brands and social media. How do you get information about the popularity of your content on major social networks? To do this you need to use special tools available in Ahrefs and Buzzsumo. If you're interested in finding a mention of your Brand, free tools like Google Alerts will come in handy. At the same time, you can turn to specialized services that monitor the internet for you.

7.4 Conclusions, cases, and recommendations

SEO is one of the most comprehensive tools of Internet marketing. It is essential to work within all of the pyramid levels, avoid mistakes, and try not to manipulate and cheat them algorithms.

What do I need to do to get traffic and access to search engines?

Let's redraw our pyramid based on the concrete steps you need to take.

1. SEO audit and its implementation is the very first and most crucial step. Most developers distance themselves from SEO. An SEO audit's primary goal is for a site to meet a search engine's requirements and eliminate fundamental problems of search engine security.

The SEO audit process will:

- Make sure server responses are correctly configured
- Make recommendations for improving site speed
- Confirm that the analysis of the site index was checked
- It tells you about errors that were found and fixed
- It tells you which technical internal duplicates have been removed
- It shows you rewritten and unique meta tags (titles and descriptions)

Further SEO results directly depend on how much and how quickly the audit will be implemented. Quite often, even the SEO audit implementation can provide a significant boost in search traffic. For example, a site for children's toys tripled its organic traffic six months after implementing an SEO audit.

2. Content strategy and content plan. Content on the internet is king, but in the case of SEO, it's not just words. A well-developed content strategy and a clear content plan can give you a lot of strong SEO benefits such as:

- Unique content
- Reach and traffic from low-frequency requests due to search requests such as «How to do ...?» and «What do you mean ..?»
- Attracting natural links and social signals
- Improvement of behavioral factors

We actively use all this in our academy, and every year we get 3-4 times more organic traffic.

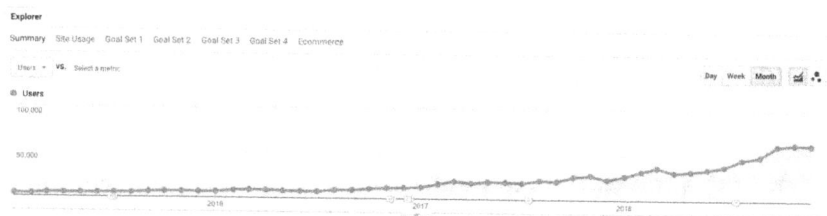

Take the time to understand what content your audience needs and set up production and distribution.

3. Keyword research. Collecting and analyzing keywords is a complex, painstaking process, but you can find pearls in the sand when you do it right. Regularly search for new keywords and reconsider your attitude towards old ones. When a job search site came to us for promotion, its SEO strategy was based on copying two main competitors. We decided to change their promoted keywords, increasing the conversion rate in applicant registrations by 33%.

4. Link-building strategy. Links can be built up by several people or departments, but they must have a joint approach; otherwise, the likelihood of being penalized by search engines is exceptionally high.

A link strategy should answer the questions:

- Where to get links from?
- What parameters are you using?
- What frequency are you using?
- What will the anchor text be?

5. Usability audit, PR, and SMM strategies are not entirely responsible for great SEO, but at the same time, they do play a role in helping your site reach a higher position.

Let's take a look at how these things work in detail using the example of our client's online store, which specializes in selling low-voltage equipment such as stabilizers and generators.

This project began with a comprehensive SEO audit, and the following tasks were carried out :

- Filters pages were blocked
- Search pages were changed
- We fixed problems with duplicates
- The URL structure was changed
- The list of keywords was expanded.
- New landing pages were created.
- Automatic and manual optimization of meta tags was implemented

Further work was done to improve the content. We formed a content plan based on the search demand analysis we did, and from that information, we added the necessary titles and categories. Particular emphasis was placed on video marketing. The videos we posted on YouTube were placed on all the site's pages. The videos were designed to do two things: encourage product reviews and give the visitors answers to popular questions, which were formulated based on the search demand on Google and YouTube. The video content that we created played the most crucial role in our campaign. It formed the basis of communication on our social networks and in our newsletters. The video content also helped increase users' time on the site pages and, most importantly, increased conversion.

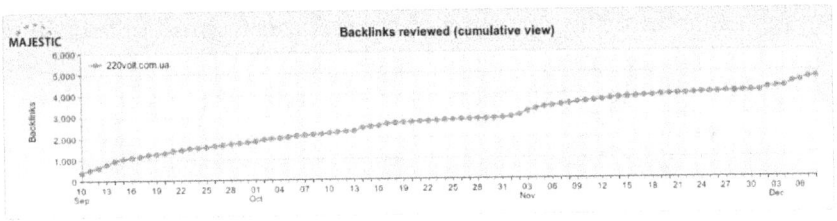

A link strategy was formed based on thematic sites, forums, and external content marketing.

These were the results:

- Traffic grew from 0 to 50 thousand a month
- The number of calls from organic searches grew by three times year to year
- Due to the content strategy, the conversion rate doubled

Still don't believe you need effective SEO? Look at your competitors' traffic data by using SimilarWeb, and your opinion will change.

7.5 SEO Checklist

1. Conduct a competitive analysis using Similarweb and Serpstat.
2. Create traffic goals for the year
3. Check the site for search engine penalties and install Google Search Console. Look for notifications in the «Violation» tabs. If you run into any problems, turn to an SEO agency for help.
4. Check the site for accessibility and speed problems

- Make sure that there are no Search Console errors
- Make sure the main pages loading speeds are at least 3 seconds (by using Pingdom Tools or any other tools with the same capabilities)
- Check for «mobility» via g.co/mobile-friendly

5. Form the structure of your site
6. Collect your keywords and place them in the appropriate pages and sections. Choose keywords based on:

- The results of your brainstorming session
- Actual data from Google Analytics and Google Search Console
- Estimated data from Google Ads Keyword Planner
- Data from the keywords of competitors from SEMRush, Serpstat, Similarweb, and other tools
- Google Trends to understand the seasonality of certain keywords

SEO (Search engine optimization) | 73

7. Optimize content on pages based on the selected keywords:

- Text on the page
- Meta Title
- Meta description
- URL

For larger projects, work with programmers to build an automatic filling system for meta tags that follow the prepared templates.

8. Analyze the duplicated content and form a plan to rewrite and replace it.

- Find plagiarism using Copyscape
- Work with an SEO specialist to eliminate internal duplicates
- Write DMCA complaints about people who stole your content
- Make a plan for rewriting content

9. Utilize Serpstat by developing a content plan, using search words and hints from search questions.

10. Do a link analysis of your competitors using Ahrefs and Majestic. Necessary information is as follows:

- Number of external links
- Number of referring domains
- Anchor distribution
- Growth dynamics.

11. Form a plan for building links based on the data of your competitive analysis. Your plan should include:

- Strategy for external content marketing
- Link building
- Work with reference exchanges (optional)

12. Analyze monthly indicators for:

- An improved position on primary keyword searches;
- An increase in reference mass;
- An increase in organic Google traffic
- An increase in Conversions and orders from organic traffic

WebPromoExperts Link analysis

Do an analysis to understand the position dynamics for the primary keyword searches.

Analysis of link growth trends

The number of links/domains as of December 1, 2019 - 23104/673
Number of links/domains as of January 1, 2020 - 23720/694

Organic traffic by Google. Conversions and orders from organic traffic

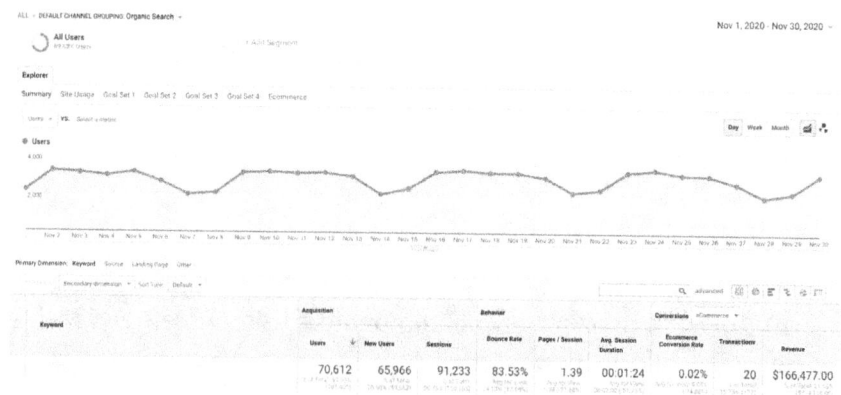

List of useful SEO tools

Services from Google

Google Search Console https://search.google.com/search-console/

Google Alerts (monitoring of new mentions)

Google Trends (analysis of keywords by season) http://www.google.com/trends/

Complaints about spam in Google SERP http://support.google.com/bin/static.py?hl=ru&ts=1114905&page=ts.cs

DMCA Report (Content Theft Complaint) https://www.google.com/webmasters/tools/dmca-notice?pli=1&&rd=1

Website responsiveness test https://testmysite.thinkwithgoogle.com/

Analytics and competitive analysis services
Similarweb https://www.similarweb.com/
SEMRush http://semrush.com/
Serpstat http://serpstat.com/

Technical Analysis Services
Analysis of website loading speed https://tools.pingdom.com/
Service for regular monitoring of the site availability status https://uptimerobot.com/

Link analysis services
Ahrefs (leader in link analysis) https://ahrefs.com/
Majestic (the second-largest link analysis service) http://majestic.com/

Chapter 8
Paid traffic

8.1 Benefits of PPC
8.2 What does PPC advertising help with?
8.3 Principles of PPC advertising
8.4 Checklist for launching PPC

8.1 Benefits of PPC

You have already answered the questions: where you are, who your target audience is, what product or service you offer, and how you will measure the results from a campaign. Now let's move onto PPC advertising and its benefits.

Paid traffic is a digital marketing tool that allows you to quickly evaluate the effectiveness of all your hypotheses about whether a product will be sold successfully and whether you understand your target audience. PPC advertising can provide insight into a potential customer's mind at every stage of the decision funnel. Paid traffic is available on most advertising platforms.

Why do I love PPC so much? Because of how effective it is at targeting your audience. You can use Google, and Facebook features to target a specific gender, age, interest, location, and keyword. You can even set a specific launch time for an advertising campaign. Most user information is found by analyzing their behavior on the internet, so make sure you use the features available on ad platforms to target them better.

The second advantage of PPC advertising is speed. You can start PPC advertising quickly, and you can stop it quickly. If someone were to launch an offline advertising campaign (television, radio), it could take months to set up. PPC advertising can be launched within 24 hours.

You can stop the advertising even quicker. One-click, and your ads are no longer shown. This can come in handy, for example, if your product is out of stock. One-click and your advertisement will disappear!

PPC advertising is one of the most reliable tools for attracting an audience on the internet. Other services struggle to achieve the same results as PPC advertising. For example, Google Adwords because it's based on the number of clicks you receive. One of the phobias that almost every advertiser has is whether an ad will be clicked. My competitors start their day by going through search results and actively clicking on all the ads they can find. Google and other large search engines that allow advertisements have a dedicated team of specialists who help keep track of these types of people and block them if they suspect fraud.

PPC advertising is suitable for any business of any size. The ability to re-contact a customer through remarketing is one of the most powerful PPC advertising tools. Remarketing is an opportunity to direct an audience that you have had already back to your site. If you've ever got the feeling that ads are following you, you are right. Banners from certain sites will follow you and try to entice you to return to them. This is remarketing, and the best part is, it's customizable on almost all advertising platforms. This tool is indispensable if you want to tell the audience about a new promotion, product, and service or if you just want to sell something.

One of the most tangible benefits of PPC advertising is that you can calculate the effectiveness. You can estimate the return on how much money you have invested, and you can also track how many calls, requests, and customer inquiries you have received.

8.2 What does PPC advertising help with?

The main thing PPC advertising helps with is increasing sales., we can expect the following things from PPC advertising:
1. Traffic
2. Leads
3. Branding
4. Recognition
5. Re-contact.

I will now go into detail about how PPC tools can help you with these things.

Search ads

Search ads appear on Google when you type in a specific question that interests you. For example, let's say you decided to learn about PPC advertising. You type in «PPC advertising courses», and an ad appears for WebPromoExperts. This is the most relevant answer to your expectations. You wanted to see information about PPC courses, and you received it. Such an answer has the maximum likelihood of an advertiser getting a sale since we did not impose ourselves on you and we helped you solve your problem. You went to the site, looked at the courses, saw they fit your price range, and you placed an order. This type of scenario produces the most conversions since it provides an answer to the user's problem. At the same time, this format is more competitive and does not always pay off since the cost of acquisition is so high.

Google Display Network (GDN) - building awareness

The second tool that allows you to generate demand is the Google Display Network. The GDN places banner and text ads for your product on Google partner sites and platforms. If you want to build awareness for a product that a potential client has no knowledge of, this is a great pay-per-click format to follow because it enables you to still reach a large audience.

Youtube - building a brand

You have to think of YouTube as a video advertising platform because it is the most popular video hosting website in the world, and it is the second most popular search engine. YouTube allows you to use video ads, banner overlays, embedded video clips (preview format), and it informs a potential customer about your product. You can also use ads on the YouTube homepage and on the YouTube embedded playlists to increase your media presence.

Remarketing and returning the audience to your site

This advertising tool is used for re-communication. By using remarketing, you can bring an audience back to your site.

Remarketing is based on two things: People who have already visited your site and your list of customer contacts. Once a user has visited your site, you can remarket to him at a later time. When you have a user's contact, you can upload this information to a separate list within your database, and then your advertising system will show the user an advertisement.

Remarketing is extremely effective at helping your client at every stage of the buying process. By using the GDN and YouTube, a user will always be aware of your product, and as a result, they can easily find you and buy from you when they are ready. Remarketing is one of the most powerful re-communication tools out there, and it helps solve the following problems for businesses:

- Informing a potential customer about a product
- Branding a product
- Reconnecting with a previous customer

If you have a new product or promotional offer, remarketing is one of the most effective tools for delivering it to your audience. For an easier way to «stalk» your audiences, you'll need administrator access privileges to your Google Analytics account, and then you will need to link it to your AdWords account.

After going through the path: Managing / Setting up an audience / Audience in Google Analytics, you have the opportunity to create the necessary lists for collecting visitors.

Important! Even if you don't plan to launch this type of ad anytime soon, we recommend creating an audience remarketing system right now so that the data can be used for later use.

Examples lists would be:

- All users
- Users who visited a specific product category
- Users who made a conversion

When setting up Google Ads, you can select any number of audiences and combine them, or highlight where they intersect.

What are the most effective remarketing strategies?
1. Talking about a new product.
If you have a new product or service, tell your existing audience about it. Selling to someone who knows about you is much easier than selling to a stranger.

2. Give discounts

If you want to offer a discount to an audience that was on your site but did not buy anything, use remarketing.

3. Tell your audience about promotions

Do you have a special offer? Make a special New Year or company anniversary offer and tell your audience about it.

We used remarketing for a promotional campaign for an online store that sells generators. As a result, our investment return was two times greater than that of the regular search campaigns.

4. Offer free content

At the WebPromoExperts Academy, remarketing is actively used to promote our events, webinars, and seminars. Let's say we were to have a person who viewed our SEO course page but did not place an order. We would then invite them to a search engine optimization webinar or SEO online conference. This would increase the chances of making a sale later on.

5. Show content based on audience interests

It is important to remarket in places where the interest is high. Our client, HeadHunter, remarkets to people who have looked at their marketing vacancies section.

6. Do not chase those who do not read your Facebook newsletters

Upload the list of inactive emails from your mailing list to the audience list on Facebook and remind them that there is a letter in the mail.

Remarketing by no means solves all the customer retention problems. Still, it can increase your conversion rate when used in conjunction with such tools as email marketing, push notifications, and SMS messages.

8.3 Principles of PPC advertising

The logic of PPC advertising is based on bidding and quality scores.

What is an auction? Auctions are the basis of PPC advertising. Whoever bets higher plays better. Classic auctions will determine how much you will pay per click or 1000 impressions when using PPC advertising.

Let's say you place a $2 bet for an advertisement, and your competitor places a $3 bet for their advertisement. If the only determining factor for ranking was the price, then the advertiser who is willing to pay $ 3 would be shown ahead of the one who was only willing to pay $2. But luckily, it is not that simple. Your ad's position in search results is based on two metrics: cost per click (how much you are willing to pay per click) and the quality of your advertisement. Google uses a scale of 1-10 to rate your advertisement.

If you did a good job on an advertising campaign, you'd get a 10. If your campaign is bad, you might get a 1,2 or 3. You can influence where you appear in PPC advertising results not only with money but also with the help of an auction. So how does a search ad auction work? A person first performs a search, Google Ads, ranks the ads, taking into account the quality score and the level of bids, and then the ads are shown. Quality Score is a keyword metric that Google gives you based on several important criteria, such as expected CTR, ad relevance, and landing page quality.

The main metrics are CTR and how many people have visited your ad. A quality score is not given to a whole campaign but a specific ad. This metric is calculated by dividing clicks by impressions and then multiplying that number by 100%. For example, your ad was clicked ten times, and it made 100 impressions. 10/100 = 0.1 (10%)

What influences CTR?

Targeting Accuracy - The more accurately you target your target audience, the higher your click-through rate will be.

Ad quality- You can write a text with grammatical errors, or you can give it to a copywriter. You can draw a banner yourself, or you can order it from a designer. A Video can be shot with a 0.3-megapixel camera, or you can contact a professional studio that will make a video for you. Your CTR will be greatly influenced by how good your ad quality is.

The relevance of the ad- How well the keywords you're using for your ads match the ad text and the site you're leading your audience to.

Technical metrics- Landing page mobility, website loading speed, and many other technical factors play a role in ad ranking.

The better you engage a person in your ad and the more it matches their interests, the higher CTR you will get. As a result, you will pay less for ads.

Launching your first Google Ads campaign

At this time, you should have solid information from your competitive analysis, the portraits of your audience should be formed, your conversion tracking should be configured in your analytics, and there should be an algorithm in place for tracking the sources of your calls. If you have done all of these things, I want to congratulate you on a job well done. You have now reached the stage where you can start setting up and launching your advertising campaign. We will now go over the principles of launching an advertising campaign in Google. Why only principles and not a step-by-step system? Because Google changes its interface 2-3 times a year. So, if I were to give you a step-by-step guide, this book would only be of use to you for a couple of months.

Starting PPC search advertising. Building the campaign structure.

The first thing to think about when launching an advertising campaign in Google Ads is what you want to advertise about your products and what you do not. Understanding the campaign structure and having a clear outline of keywords by page will allow you to save a significant amount of time.

The maximum fragmentation of an advertising account is not always justified. Potential improvements in conversions are not offset by the complexity of the campaign. It is necessary to strongly think about whether to split into different regions and devices.

List the main categories and subcategories of your products and services because they will form your advertising campaign structure.

Keyword research

We examined the logic of keyword selection in detail in the SEO chapter. The approaches and tools are the same, so we will not go over them again. Let's take a look at what differentiates keyword approaches in SEO and PPC advertising. The main thing to pay attention to is the types of keywords that are matching. This setting allows you to expand or narrow the reach of your ad.

There are four types of keyword matching available in Google Ads:

- Exact
- Phrase
- Broad with a modifier
- Broad

The smallest match type in Google Ads is exact matching. When setting up advertising, phrases are indicated by square brackets, for example, [buy an apartment]. Using this match type, you will only be shown requests for things that you have specified. This works well when you already have your ad campaign results data, and you know the keywords that have the best conversion rates.

There are plenty of problems with exact matches. The main issue with exact matches is that the cost is high, and so is this competition. You can get out of this trap with more encompassing match types like the phrase match type, which is denoted by its use of double-quotes. By specifying «Buy an apartment» in the settings, you will receive ad impressions for all keywords where this phrase is presented. For example, «I want to **buy an apartment** in installments.»

The maximum reach is given by the broad and broad with modifier match types. In the first case, when people ask to buy an apartment, you will appear for all phrases containing: misspellings and even synonyms and relevant options. The broad match type with a modifier will also give ample opportunities, but without the base of synonyms. It is phrases and broad matching types that allow you to cover the long keyword tails to the maximum. But there are some potential negative outcomes that you have to consider. You can start to be shown in search requests that produce no sales and sometimes even have nothing to do with you.

To avoid showing unnecessary phrases, you must use the negative keyword setting. By adding other cities, older houses, and brands of competitors to your list, you will avoid being shown to people who will never become your paying customers. **Important!** 25% of Google requests are never repeated, so a keyword list must be constantly updated. Finding and updating negative keywords is a must and is a critical part of the battle for an effective ad campaign.

Ads

You already have a list of keywords that you want to advertise with, as well as a clear understanding of which pages you will lead your audience to and what match type you will use. It's now time to get started with the advertisements.

Below is what you need to include to distinguish yourself from a dozen or more competitors and bring a person to your site, and then close the deal.

Our recommendations in this matter are quite simple:

1. A good USP. Each ad should contain your unique selling proposition. If all advertising messages contain the same message, the likelihood of getting a client is extremely low. For the USP formation, we will need all the previously prepared works like competitive analysis, character portraits, etc.

2. Call to action. No matter how loudly your USP speaks about itself, it's always a good idea to push the user towards what exactly you want them to do. Include terms like buy, register, and download in your advertisements.

3. Figures. Usually, numbers are part of the USP, but at the same time, numbers can be used to make positive statements about your product or service. For example, we have had over 300 satisfied customers, and we have been in business since 1992. Numbers can be a really good anchor point that attracts the attention of your potential client.

4. Special offer. If you have a promotion or discount for new customers, do not hesitate to tell them about it in your ad. Information about promotions will increase the click-through rate and conversion rate of your ads. According to the statistics of our advertising campaigns, WebPromoExperts has an 80-110% increase in the conversion of ads per promotional month.

5. Giveaways. You can try to give pieces of your product to your clients for free to entice them to buy from you. If you have a gift for your audiences, like free content or a free event, tell potential customers

about it. Offering free events will almost always yield higher conversion rates. We get 30-40% conversion rates from registrations at free events. This allows us to build a community and build a base for email marketing.

6. Keyword entry. You've probably noticed that when your request matches the ad text, it is highlighted in bold. Of course, this makes it more visible. I recommend that you figure out how the dynamic keyword insertion ad feature works because it will automatically add keywords to your ads.

7. Ad extensions. This concise ad format forces us to train our writing talent, but much more useful additional information can be added in the ad extensions.

I recommend using the following extensions:

- Addresses and telephone numbers
- Additional links (leads to other sections)
- Structured descriptions
- Prices
- Reviews

No one single technique that I have recommended will guarantee you success. You will get real results only by experimenting with all of these options.

8.4 Checklist for launching PPC

When launching your Google Ads campaign, check the following points:

1. **Make sure your Google Ads and Google Analytics accounts are linked** and that automatic link tagging with GCLID (Google Click ID) is enabled. If this is not done, traffic from Google Ads will be displayed as analytics traffic from SEO (google / organic). You will then not be able to assess the effectiveness of your advertising campaign

2. Check that the structure of the advertising campaigns/groups corresponds to your site structure

3. You must have separate search and display campaigns

4. Optimal name for the campaign domain_network_location_category

5. The budget is limited and distributed across campaigns

6. Brand requests are highlighted in a separate campaigns

7. Display campaigns limit the frequency of impressions to one user

8. Each ad group has at least 3-5 ads

9. Ads use a call to action

10. Campaigns use different types of keyword matching

11. Must have formed and constantly reviewed negative keywords lists

12. Google Ads extensions are used (addresses and phone numbers, quick links, reviews)

Chapter 9
SMM - Promotion in social networks

9.1 Why go to social media?
9.2 SMM pitfalls
9.3 Social media promotion tools

- Why go to social networks?
- SMM pitfalls
- Analysis of competitors in social networks
- Social media analytics
- Content plan
- Promotion tools
- Working with negative reviews
- Social Media Promotion Checklist

Today, promotion in social networks has a special visual appeal. When advertising outside of social networks, you have to pay a big sum of money. Promotion on social networks makes sense because your audience is always there.

9.1 Why go to social media?

The first reason to advertise on social media is to have a large reach. Social networks are among the most popular sites in any country. People love to socialize, have fun, and follow what is happening in the lives of others.

What exactly will be sold on social media?
Before answering this question, let's think about why users come to social networks. If we go to search engines for answers to questions, then what is the main motive for visiting Facebook?

The answers are clear and simple:

1. Communication and networking. We want to keep in touch with old acquaintances and make new useful acquaintances.

2. Fun. Fun and positive emotions are some of the main reasons why memes and postcards will continue to move from virtual life to real life.

3. Self-development. We want to better ourselves by frequently tracking industry communities, opinion leaders, and other social media experts who have the same interests as us.

Looking at this list, you can immediately guess several business areas that can easily sell their goods and services through social networks.

1. Gifts and everything related to the fun
2. Courses, educational seminars, conferences
3. Interest clubs, communities
4. Dating services

Feeling disappointed that you didn't see your business on this list? Don't worry! Two universal methodologies can help any business.

Methodology 1: Strong visual and emotional presentation. You are not selling customers a product or service; you're selling them the euphoric feeling of ownership. If you can entice a person to buy your product by just having them look at your proposal, you will increase your chances of making a sale. Tours, jewelry, cars, and real estate are amazing at generating customers based on this principle.

Methodology 2: Discount or gift. Social media users have been burned a lot, but they still will take a chance on a good deal. You will acquire a couple of thousand subscribers on your page by using this method, and by bringing these people to your site, you will get a customer base for future work. All sorts of contests and sweepstakes in social networks work in the same way. It is difficult to sell a car in an economic crisis. If you want to entice them, offer them a free test drive. A person will not buy Spanish courses right away, but if we give a free test and disappoint him a little with the results, the chances of an emotional purchase are higher. Social media is one of the most powerful tools to bring a prospect to you for a «free test drive.»

Discounts are great and give a crazy return, especially on certain special days. Special days like Black Friday and New Year's provide great opportunities to really increase your sales!

By combining a strong emotional-visual presentation with discounts and free content, you can create a great deal of social media buzz. More likely than not, this will become one of your main customer acquisition tools for your website.

9.2 SMM pitfalls

Let's look at the two most difficult things about SMM; low organic reach and spam.

Low organic reach
One reason why so many website owners and entrepreneurs rush to social media is for the seemingly free tool. It all seems pretty easy, right? You sit, post various information in a feed, collect many likes and comments, and everyone who saw your post then may buy something from you. It sounds great, but in reality, it's not that simple. The problem is that Facebook, Instagram, Twitter, and other social platforms are also businesses. Platforms also want to make money from advertising. Algorithms for displaying information in a feed are designed in such a way that when information is posted on a company page, only a small part of your existing subscribers will see it. How? They subscribed to us! Yes, they might have subscribed to you, but you can only get 100% message visibility by resorting to advertising within the network. And the cost of advertising on Facebook is not much lower than in search engines and even higher when compared to other channels. The first problem that novice promoters face on social networks is that a seemingly free promotion works with only 10-20% of the already assembled audience. For your message to be seen by everyone, you need to click the «Give money to Facebook» (Boost post) button under each post.

Spam
The second problem largely stems from the first. Not getting the desired result when working with your audience and not being sure of your advertising's effectiveness can lead you to the dark side. You probably received invitations to all kinds of groups and events that you have already heard about. Would you write a personal message to some distant acquaintances or someone you just added to your friend's list asking them to like or share a post? No, you wouldn't. It would be

considered strange if you did. When businesses do this, people will consider it spam, and there is only a small chance that they will take your product seriously. In addition to spam, there are also many other grey area methods businesses use. Mass following (adding friends and subscribing to a potential audience), mass liking (creating interest in a potential client by spamming his activities), and inviting (inviting to subscribe to a page where you have a choice to subscribe or not) are all grey area methods that businesses use to promote themselves.

Where to begin?

The last couple of paragraphs may have upset you, and now you might be tempted to skip to another section. Don't! With the right approach, social networks can bring you 10-50% of your total traffic! The logic of working with social networks goes hand in hand with our questions: Where? What for? Who! How? What's the best? You must understand the content rules in social networks and address all these questions.

What content drives competitors?

The first thing we will decide on is which social network gives competitors more traffic. Let me remind you that we are looking for a measurable result, and it is only possible to find measurable results by looking at this process as a chain of events. Our old friend SimilarWeb.com will help you find the social channel that your competitors are paying attention to the most. This will also give you an idea of what needs to be monitored first.

By referring to the statistics of your Facebook page, you can get answers to the following questions:

1. How many posts do you need to make a week to get subscribers?

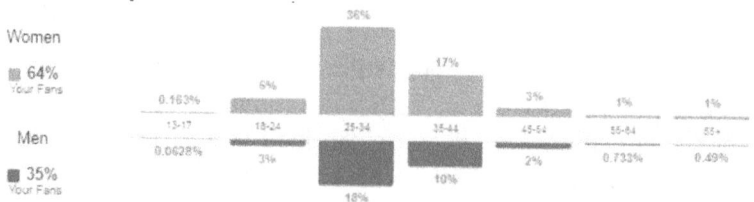

Going to the admin panel of your Facebook business page, you immediately get an answer to the first question about the possible number of publications. This is not a magic number that a super-secret algorithm determines, but just an ordinary evaluation that is done with a handy summary of statistics.

By going to the People tab, you will see statistics on how your audience's interest is distributed by days of the week and times of the day.

Now we must figure out what competitor content has garnered the most shares. BuzzSumo and Ahrefs Content Explorer can help you figure this out.

For example, here are last month's most popular WebPromoExperts repost pages.

What's next?
Do you have an understanding of what others are doing and how you will differentiate from them? Good! The next important step in creating your social media promotion will be a well-formed KPI system for yourself and your colleagues. In the analytics section, we built a table, let's adapt it for social networks. What result would you like to get by starting a promotion in social networks? Sales, of course. But the main problem is that social networks primarily work off of loyalty, community, and feedback, not sales. So the question now is, how do you link sales to what is happening on your social media platforms? We have gone over this part in the web analytics chapter; you will need to be patient. Reports on conversions from social media traffic must be

supplemented with data from the main micro-conversions (subscriptions to the newsletter, registrations on the site), as well as the assisted conversions.

Formation of a content plan

The basis of any activity on social media is content. We examined the logic of content marketing in detail, let's adapt it now for social networks. Direct selling can only be done for a limited number of topics. You will have to build trust and prove that you are worthy for the rest.

The forming of a content plan is based on the PNP principle. There are three categories of content to help you sell on social media:

- Professional
- News
- Personal

Professional – you should want to show your expertise. Only in the very beginning will it seem that your expert opinion on shut-off valves or internal site optimization is a useless thing that no one needs. I assure you that it is not. It is important to remember that we write and pass content not through the prism of ourselves but through the portraits that you drew in the previous chapter. It seems that installing doors or assembling a kitchen is a trifling matter that anyone can do. Still, people who are currently experiencing the torment of repairing their house will gladly thank you with a like for good advice on a topic such as this.

Professional content includes:

- Training materials
- Manuals in the format of «How to do it yourself?»
- Interviews
- Research
- Checklists
- Strategies

All this can take place in the following formats:

- Articles
- Videos
- Infographics

- Live videos and online broadcasts

It should be noted that the most difficult thing for a business is the production of professional content, but it is this that gives you the most return.

News content
News content only requires the correct analysis of information flows. As of right now, some event is probably happening in your area. The same goes for events in almost all niches. Your task should be to present the audience with the most valuable information possible.

News content includes:

- Industry news
- Partner news
- Announcements of industry events

Personal content
I would advise you to keep your content professional. Personal content should only be used if it validates your expertise or helps you secure a loyal, friendly community.

A separate viable category of personal content is the so-called Social Proof content (social confirmation). Essentially, all content in this category is a beautifully presented portfolio that includes:

- Customer reviews
- A detailed description of the work (case studies)
- Success stories
- Interviews with clients

How would you go further? By providing at least half of your content in your professional feeds, you will be pleasantly surprised by the results of your promotions on social networks.

What are the formats?
If we're talking about the content formats of social networks, their virality is already predetermined at the start by the algorithms of social networks. Let's take a look at Facebook algorithms and the organic reach of posts on the Facebook network. Organic reach is the

percentage of subscribers who have seen your post. This on average is 10% of your subscribers, but this figure can vary significantly depending on the content.

Let's take a look at the most popular post formats in descending order of organic reach:

- Text
- Post-link
- Images
- Videos and gifs
- Live videos

Text posts have the lowest organic reach at 1-2 %. People on social media don't like a lot of letters, and the reaction to text content clearly illustrates this. Use Fewer letters and more colors and emotions. For us, link posts are the most desirable for driving traffic to our sites. Social networks do not particularly approve of an audience's withdrawal from their platform, and businesses are typically punished with an extremely low organic reach of about 1-2%.

Images- In some communities, there is a feeling that nothing other than graphic content can exist. Graphics have been a favorite for a long time, and even now, a vibrant image with a clear call to action can give your post organic reach equal to or greater than that of a video. Expect 3-5% of your reach from images.

Video and online streaming is the format that is flooding social networks. Everyone in the marketing community swears by view counters, and yes, video + streams have the maximum virality. 10% is what you can generally expect. Remember that you will most likely not stick to one format, so include several content formats in your content plan at once.

What can you do to increase your organic reach?

Most of the social media promotion activities revolve around increasing reach. Without paying the platform, make sure that as many people see your messages as possible. This is task number one. To do this, you need to understand which social network metrics can help the most with organic reach. These are shares, comments, and likes, in that order of importance.

Shares - when a person has shared your message in their feed, it adds to your page's reach. Shares have the biggest impact on organic reach. Shares are popularized contests and giveaways. All sorts of prizes are given, from discount coupons to outright fraudulent deals for apartments and cars. This is how a separate category of social media users appeared. The marketing community calls these guys prize-winners. For them, contests are a kind of lottery that boosts their adrenaline and gives them a rush. If this type of person does not win, he and his friends might leave a few nasty comments on your page. Contests aimed at getting shares and subscribers have received several administrative restrictions in social networks. To get shares is very difficult, but it is possible!

Comments - Comments are the second most powerful tool for increasing organic reach. The more active your comment sections are, the more your posts will pop up in people's feeds. If the post is controversial or can be debated, an online battle may ensue in your comments, further increasing your post's likelihood of reaching more people. I also recommend the age-old technique of asking someone to put a + or - as a sign of agreement or disagreement. This can help kickstart your comment section.

Likes - There wouldn't be such a thing as a social network without likes, but at the same time, they have a lot less important in comparison with comments and shares. Now that you possess the necessary understanding of how everything works, you can proceed to the most interesting part; promoting content.

9.3 Social media promotion tools

When we talk about promotion, the first thing to come to many people's minds are the gray area methods that we previously discussed. In this book, we will only work with legitimate methods.

These are the three ways to promote SMM:

- Paid advertising
- Work with opinion leaders
- Work with communities

Let's start with paid advertising. Without it, breaking through the algorithms of social networks is difficult. The possibility of targeting the audience correctly is high here. You can target your audience by gender, age, interest, location, link, and audience list. Creating similar audiences based on lists you already have is also a great strategy to employ.

In our experience, the effectiveness of targeting looks like this (from best to worst):

1. Targeting existing subscribers
2. Targeting Friends Subscribers
3. Databases for audience remarketing on a site and databases from CRM (phone numbers and email)
4. Targeting by interests as close to your topic as possible.

If we talk about the effectiveness of advertising formats, then such a gradation will look like this:

- Posts in the feed
- Stories on Facebook and Instagram
- Partner networks
- Etc

Facebook has over 20 different places for ads. Paid advertising on social media platforms work especially well in conjunction with promotions. For example, our client, who sells furniture advertised on Facebook and Instagram during Black Friday. He then got a return on his investment of 1 to 157.

Working with opinion leaders and communities

Promotion on social networks is a fight for people's opinions. Who can convince them better than the people they follow?

Opinion leaders are bloggers, journalists, experts in various industries, and celebrities. When your idol recommends a campaign or brand from his page, this is a strong reason to learn more about the product and perhaps even use it. You can work with opinion leaders by following three old, world-proven schemes.

1. **Be friends-** You know them personally. You know the names of their children and share common hobbies. Do you think they will refuse you if you ask them to share something for you when you are announcing a new product?

2. **Barter** - Invite the influencer to use your product in exchange for public feedback. This is a popular format. Auto brands, for example, are not at all opposed to a lengthy test drive for journalists and bloggers in exchange for feedback about them.

3. **Money** - Everything is clear here. You start your meeting with an understandable question: «How much?» You negotiate a little then you make a deal. You receive what you want, and you pay them for their services.

Working with communities
Communities are a collective intelligence controlled by a moderator. My wife is now on maternity leave, and one of the Facebook groups she's in has 10 thousand mothers in it. It is often the source of answers to questions such as:

- Which stroller to buy?
- What is a good orthopedic surgeon?
- Which bike is better for a one-and-a-half-year-old girl?

All questions have specific commercial implications. Most often, moms like her come to the discussion thread with their suggestions, experience, and recommendations. But who prevents representatives of commercial brands from pushing their content in these spaces?

The person who you need to make friends, barter, and negotiate with within these communities is the moderator.

Reputation management and working with negative reviews
In terms of influencing reputation and spreading negativity, social networks play a vital role. Social networks can give your product or service short-term glory. Once word gets out that your no product is no good, your sales will cease to exist.

There are several important milestones that you need to consider to prepare for this:

- Marketing
- PR
- Search Engine Reputation Management

At the marketing stage, you must recognize your weaknesses and minimize their impact on your promotion. The task of marketing is to quickly respond to external calls and turn disadvantages into advantages. If the product is bad, the audience will tell you, and this sentiment will spread like wildfire if not properly dealt with. Next comes the role of PR. How should we react to bad PR? Most reactions to negativity are not very forward-thinking.

Ignoring negative feedback

People that use social networks can be very unforgiving. Ignoring negative feedback is a fast way to destroy a product. Should we just delete it then? Also not an option. A text message has a lower organic reach than a picture. After you delete the comment, it will come back to life as a screenshot, which is even worse than the original comment. «It's not us, it's you. You are all lying. This is also a road to nowhere, and I hope you understand that. In this situation, search engine reputation management and a social media post-response team are like two janitors trying to clean all of New York City by themselves. But this is only the case if you are not trying to improve your product.

To start a normal process of working with reviews, you should first start to monitor them. You can check the review yourself or with the help of the Google Alerts service. It can also be automatic if you are willing to pay. Services such as Buzzsumo or BrandMention are great paid services you can use to monitor reviews. You will receive regular notifications when the system finds a review about you. OK! We found out what they wrote about us. The next course of action is to determine if the comment is negative or positive.

If it's a positive comment- Say «thank you» and try to remember this person. He or she can be a brand advocate in the future.

Neutral comment - Give a like and move on.

Negative - And here appears the notorious negativity of the internet. What do we do?

Let's start by defining the type of negativity:
1. Constructive
2. Black PR
3. Irrational
4. Trolling

You usually have to deal with a mix of these negatives. Let me give you a simple example. Several years ago, our competitor decided to place a promotional campaign (order an online promotion from us and get such and such gifts) on a trade publication. There was a comment made by a user who announced the company's dishonesty. Ignoring common sense by not taking their promotion down, the agency director proceeded to argue with the user in the comments. The trolls came running in and began to teach him a lesson about life and business management. Several other customer reviews were also clearly black PR. How did it all end? More than 500 comments appeared on the post. 500! The article ranked first on Google for the keyword «company name reviews» and second for the company name.

You will have to deal with constructive criticism when you do not live up to your current or potential clients' expectations. With constructive criticism, everything seems so clear, and at the same time, everything becomes infinitely more complicated. You are working, working, trying, trying, and then someone comes and says that everything is bad. How does this happen? The hardest thing to do in this line of work is to turn off your emotions. Try to help the client solve his problem and return their money if the situation cannot be resolved. This amount of money will eventually be returned to you a hundredfold one way or the other. When working with negativity, there are no universal rules. I can only give you one recommendation. Try to take the negative person offline immediately by helping him. It is better to do it by phone, mail, or personal message. Do not address the situation where the post was made. Have a pre-prepared message that says you are upset by the current situation and you will do everything to solve it. The answer should not look like «Your call is very important to us .» This will just escalate the situation even further. Make sure your message shows real concern and indicates a genuine desire to help and solve the problem. Ideally, the message should not be made on behalf of a pompous brand but from a responsible employee who can realistically solve the problem. After all, no matter what, people don't trust brands; they trust people. Remember this!

After the conflict is settled, should you remove the comment? What's the point? If it is really annoying you, ask the author of the negative comment to do it for you. He most probably won't refuse you since you helped him. The second most common type of negativity is black

PR. Not everyone is going to like you; it's just a simple fact of life. Have that defamation suit locked and ready to go; you might need it. When it comes to black PR, do not procrastinate; refute it harshly and clearly. A long answer can be perceived as an agreement with the fact that there is a problem, and an indistinct position can strengthen the culprit's image. Concentrate on presenting a strong position at the start of your statement. And remember! It is necessary to refute with proportionate force. If only a couple of people are bothering you, don't make a statement on a page that's going to be read by thousands.

Irrational negativity is a challenge for everyone. For some reason, your client or potential buyer did not understand the product or service and perceived it as your problem. Here you have to muster all of the restraint you have. In this situation, it is unwise to convey that the customer was too dumb to figure out the product. Unjustified expectations are a thing that can almost never be dealt with; having said that, the problem is in the expectations themselves. Even though you have already given your best to solve such situations, you will most likely have to go above and beyond by having your best customer service manager find a solution. In these situations, such efforts will pay off, and instead of a malicious hater, you will get a brand advocate who will recommend you, love you, and support you in every possible way. In my line of work, I have students with a low level of computer literacy but a high level of eagerness to master the Internet business. By just being patient with them at the beginning of a course, I often meet their expectations later in other courses, seminars, and modular programs.

Trolling

This is a special kind of negativity. When I was young, kids had fun by just prank-calling people. Now those kids have grown up and have become uncles and aunts, but the habit of making fun of others using impunity has not passed. This is how Internet trolls are born. The only rule that can work here is not to feed the troll. Responding will only add fuel to the fire.

To briefly summarize responding to negativity:

1. Take them offline by solving the problem. Do not address the problem in the place where it happened.

2. React promptly and clearly. A delayed response and fuzzy position will give a 100% chance of the problem to continue.
3. Do not feed the trolls.
4. Try to understand the person who is upset.

The most difficult thing is to stop perceiving all strangers on social networks as trolls and ill-wishers. Start asking why they wrote what they wrote. Believe me; the results will surprise you!

What is left to do?
Social networks are the tool from which everyone expects intangible happiness and then very often gets disappointed. To ensure that you do not fall into this trap, make sure you do the following:

- Have a ready-made content plan for your pages, where at least a third and preferably half of the content is professional content
- Make sure you are ready to allocate a budget for advertising on social networks and understand how your campaign works and how you will measure its result
- You have to decide if you want to do manual or automatic monitoring. Track negative comments about you and react to them in the right way

Chapter 10
Email Marketing

10.1 Where can I get a subscriber base?
10.2 Email Marketing Checklist
Case study

Email marketing is one of the most effective tools that exist for repeat customer communication. It solves many tasks, such as getting feedback, repeating sales, building loyalty, and delivering content to the consumer.

The main problem is the association of email marketing with spam. What is the difference?

If a user has permitted you to send emails, then this is email marketing; if he did not give this permission (and you bought a database, downloaded, etc.), then this is spam.

The main ways of obtaining permission are:
1) order forms
2) subscription forms
3) exchange of business cards at exhibitions
4) questionnaires in offline stores

If you use email marketing to tell people about yourself who don't know about your existence, it will be spam. The person who gets mail from you must agree to receive any correspondence from you. The initial contact can happen offline or at your event, or it can be the purchase of your product that begins the relationship. Also, in any letter that you send to a person, there should be an unsubscribe option. Even if a person subscribes himself or left an email address for you, he may forget why he did it, and a short reminder of why he receives the letter should be in every email.

If you follow this simple logic: send the newsletter only to those who have already interacted with you through sales and attending events, your newsletter will have the right to be called email marketing. If you send emails to people who are not yet ready to receive them, it will be spam. It is important to understand that email marketing is based on content. If you want to receive positive feedback about your emails, make sure the information is useful to the user. You should not write only about your promotions, sales, and discounts (except mailings, where the promised discount became the reason for the mailing), but also share useful articles, videos, and research that other market players do not give them.

For example, we conduct free seminars in our area, and one of the letters that we can send after the seminar maybe something like this: «Thank you for being at the seminar. Would you like to buy our course? «The likelihood that a person will click «spam» on such a letter or simply ignore it is extremely high. But if the letter contains helpful e-books and videos on internet marketing, the chances that the letter will be opened and viewed is much greater. The letter should contain both a discount and an offer to buy the course. This way, you lose fewer subscriptions and gain more loyalty. The audience is then more likely to return to us again. Email marketing is not spam; it is a communication tool and part of direct marketing. It doesn't work as a standalone tool, it's part of your overall communication with your prospect.

10.1 Where can I get a subscriber base?

A question that interests everyone is: «How to make people leave their emails, and can you communicate with them?»

Existing customers
This is the VIP segment of your mailing list. Do not forget to clarify if they are opposed to such mailings.

Offer discounts
This is the way many online stores operate. For example, register, leave an email and get $5 off your first purchase. Another way of offering discounts is to give out loyalty cards.

Free content.

A person subscribes to you and, in return, receives free content such as videos, books, and checklists. On the WebPromoExperts website, by subscribing to a pop-up window that offers you to leave an email, you will receive a series of video tutorials.

Updated blog

A blog is a kind of media. People want to read and receive news on a regularly. By subscribing to a blog update, they expect to receive the most interesting news of the week, month, or another specified period.

Activities - After an event, want to receive an email and phone number.

Contests- Because a person is registered, you can communicate with them better.

Social media forms - Facebook has a special plugin that allows you to invite people to subscribe to a newsletter by leaving an email.

Registration- In addition to receiving technical letters (about payment, resetting the password), a person can receive a newsletter or digest from you by registering on your site.

Event-marketing - as a tool to attract subscribers

We are one of the best when it comes to gathering subscribers from events. We collect emails from people when they register for online conferences, webinars, free seminars, and courses. Each of these categories is a separate segment of the mailing list.

Having attended an event of a certain category, a person most likely wants to study this topic further. Suppose you build your communication correctly by sending him useful and interesting content. In that case, you can turn him, if not into a paying customer, into a loyal follower who will recommend you to all their friends and acquaintances.

Free content

Free content should be implemented by using popups in different parts of a site. The pop ups should trigger when a person wants to leave a site or close a page. Offer the user free content like an e-book in exchange for their email. Try to make the e-book match what the client is interested in.

Blog updates

This is a popular strategy to form a database. After you have decided how you will collect contacts, the important question to answer is what you will send and how often.

What should be sent?

- Useful content
- Announcements
- Reminders and notifications
- Offers and promotions

Regular mailings

Digest mailings are one of the most popular formats. What's in a digest mailing? The regular content that you have created throughout the week. It could be company news, blog posts, interesting videos, or industry news. Communication via digest is a type of content plan.

Digests can be sent out at different rates. For example, a part of your audience is less actively reading your content, so you would send them a digest once a month. Another audience might want new content regularly, and for these people, you would send newsletters once a week. The optimal mailing frequency for most companies is once a week. Statistics show that quality communication decreases the number of unsubscribes and complaints about spam.

Triggered mailings

This is one of the most effective forms of mailing list communication. Triggered mailings allow you to become friends with a person by using an automated email chain.

A person will receive a chain of letters by subscribing to your lead magnets like a free ebook. There should be a final target action like them buying a course from you at the end of this chain.

The first letter a person receives should contain an ebook. After studying it for several days or a week, he receives a second letter, in which he is offered a video about the same topic. Then there is a feedback collection process where an automatic letter asks whether the person watched the video and if they found it useful. Once the person has given feedback, another video is sent along with an offer to purchase a product at a discount. If a person does not open this letter, he is again sent another letter asking why he didn't open the previous letter.

The trigger chain can be 2, 3, or 100 interactions. The main thing to understand is the end goal and that the content you are sending out is high quality. At first, stick to sending out content that is relevant to their interests. For most businesses, there will be long chains for their products and services. The length of a chain depends on the value of the product or service that is being sold. For example, to sell a product for $200, 1 letter is enough, but if the cost of the service is $ 5,000, then more letters will be needed. How often letters are sent is determined by the time it takes to make a purchase decision. If you sell real estate and the time table for deciding to buy property is six months, you should be sending out letters one time per week for six months.

Promotional mailings

Promotional mailings or notifications about a new product are among the most effective mailings in terms of sales. The base of subscribers who regularly read your content are quite loyal people, and they have already most likely bought something from you. Selling to someone who has already bought something from you is much easier than selling to someone you have met for the first time. Therefore, if you have a promotion or additional product, let your audience know about it in the mailing list. One letter is usually ineffective; a series of several interactions usually works. For example, you decide to hold a promotion. Notify the audience about this on day one of the promotion. State that the promotion will end soon halfway through the promotion. Send 1-2 letters at the end of the promotion period. The letters that are sent at the end of the promotion are for those who did not open the previous letter or for those who clicked on your promotional link but did not place an order. Mailing list services will take care of this process for you, and they will try to find different ways to communicate with your audience whether they open your letters or not.

In our case, we have received very positive results from promotional mailings.

Reminders

People don't relate to sales letters but technical letters. For example, sending thanks for registering on a site or event and reminding them about seminars and webinars. Use reminder letters as an opportunity to try to sell something.

Segmentation

It is important that your database is segmented by interests, and you communicate with people based on what they did or did not do on your site.

We segment the database by location, event, interest, and by courses people have attended. The more you segment your audience, the more success you will have because you are giving them information that interests them, and as a result, they are less likely to unsubscribe from you.

Regularly send emails to people who do not view your mailings and ask them why. If they answer you, there might still be a way to retain the user. If the response to you reaching out is negative and they want to unsubscribe from you, honor this request.

An unsubscribe letter should say something like, «would you like to unsubscribe from the mailing list?» This type of letter will give you an insane amount of unsubscribes.

Reactivation letters should be carried out quarterly or every six months. People who do not respond should be removed from the database since it is this segment of inactive subscribers that causes filters to think you are spam. Not removing them from your database can lead to the general perception that your company's promotions are just spam and untrustworthy.

Other tools to use

SMS, retargeting using emails (if a person did not open your last letter, you can upload his email to Facebook and Google and send him a reminder), and browser push notifications work great with mailings. For us, emails and newsletters are the most powerful communication tools in terms of sales. A third of the academy's sales come from mailing lists. It is important to remember that emails are not a quick fix like any type of communication. It takes time and more than one letter before a person trusts you and buys your product.

10.2 Email Marketing Checklist

1. Mailing service
2. Contacts are segmented and distributed by lists
3. Strategy to constantly collect new subscribers:
4. There is a subscription form on the site
5. It is possible to subscribe to the site/blog updates
6. An audience with events
7. Existing and potential client
8. Content mailing plan
9. Responsibility for maintaining mailings has been allocated to an individual or team.
10. Reactivation letters are being sent out quarterly or every six months

Case study

WebPromoExperts, as an internet marketing academy, has built its brand on content. This content became the driving force in our marketing activities and brought together individual tools to form a single digital marketing system. WebPromoExperts is part of one of the biggest and most successful digital marketing agencies in Ukraine. We used our agency's wealth of knowledge to give premium lessons on digital marketing topics like search engine optimization, PPC advertising, promotion in social networks, and email marketing.

When creating our lessons, we used the same questions we taught you in this book.

1. Who am I? Mission, vision, values
2. What am I selling? Product or Service
3. Where am I in the market? Analysis of the niche and existing competitors.
4. Why do I go online? Formation of a system of performance indicators and setting up web analytics
5. Who are we targeting! Formation of a portrait of the target audience
6. What types of content work?
7. How to conduct a promotion and use seeding tools?

8. Could it be better? Internet marketer's guide to continuous improvement

Mission and product

The academy quickly adapted the agency's mission "help businesses increase online sales." Webpromo does this through its services; the academy does this by teaching entrepreneurs and specialists about the most effective promotion tools. The product line consists of 20 online educational programs. Each new product considers the feedback of its graduates, is more interactive and gives new and interesting homework assignments.

The role of market analysis

Analysis of the market, competitors, foreign content, and educational projects allows us to keep up with global digital marketing trends.

The evaluation of results

Over the past few years, we've gone a lot further than just understanding conversions in Google Analytics.

This cannot be called transactional analytics, but using a CRM, we can understand how our content activity affects sales. Thanks to the integration of Google Analytics and a CRM, we can understand what sources bring the most sales.

Content

When we started our content activity, the detailed analysis we did on our competitors was very useful. We found that there were many good blogs but few online events. This is why we started doing webinars. This format was easy for us to follow because we wrote less and talked more. Initially, our webinars only gathered about 30-40 people. Then I happened to come across the book «Content Marketing» by Stelzner. In the book, I read that your company can take off by having expert guests on your webinars. After I read this, I started meeting digital marketing experts and inviting them to host webinars. It was mutually beneficial. We help an expert become even more popular, and in turn, he leads an audience to us. This logic has stayed with us in almost all forms of content that we generate. We do webinars, online conferences, and blogs with experts. 15-20% of our information comes from us, and the other 80% comes from experts that give lectures on digital marketing and how it works. Experts give us the largest niche reach and recognition. This leads to a lot of hits on our social media.

After utilizing experts, our webinars began to be attended by 300-500 people on average.

The webinar format is great, but it is limited. You can expand your reach by inviting multiple experts to give lectures. This is how we got into doing online conferences. It differs from a webinar in its approach. You treat it like a conference, but according to its technical characteristics, it is the same as a webinar, but with a better broadcast. We hold conferences from a studio with 4 TV cameras. It is much easier to attract people, because the conference lasts all day, has a large broadcast, and the best experts speak. This format has become our calling card and helps us immensely.

By creating many forms of event content, we are also creating content for a blog. We used recordings of webinars and online conferences as part of our blog content. Then we invited experts to write about hot topics like promotion in social networks, search engines, and other formats. The blog has had over 100,000 visits to date.

Traffic

If you think about which three elements factor into creating great content, it becomes much easier to evaluate results. Without content, you will not receive traffic from emails and social networks. If you just use emails and social media for sales and special offers, your audience will burn out very quickly. If you provide useful information, then emails and social networks can build you a community that will grow quickly.

The third tool, which is completely devoid of content, is search engine optimization (SEO). You won't get traffic without search engines so you must generate quality text content. Writing quality articles is hard. At this stage, our video and webinar content activities were key. It's much easier to extract useful content from a video than writing content from scratch. If you open our analytics, you will see that about 60% of our traffic comes from these sources. Just because these tools are effective does not mean we should give up on paid advertising. Paid advertising brings us a third of our orders. We respond to the audience's interest by the use of search engines, the GDN, Facebook, and events using all types of remarketing.

In paid advertising, we also redefined the approach towards content. Direct advertising of a course gave us too high of an application cost, which forced us to look for other options. Today, the main advertising budgets go to advertising-free events like seminars, webinars, and online conferences. We make a lot of sales from this audience. A systematic approach to internet marketing and content has given us much more than just a stream of leads if you think about it. Below I have nine small case studies for you to see how digital marketing works.

Case 1. Database of contacts

From our content activity, we get traffic and a contact base of potential customers. A person who registers for an event gives at least two of his contacts: a phone number and an email. Phone numbers for salespeople are a warm base. If you call a person and say: «Let me sell you a course,» you can rest assured that he will probably hang up on you. But if you phrase the call like «Hello! You were at a webinar / online conference yesterday. Are you interested in a marketing course?» The chances are that you will not be so rudely answered even if the person is only interested in free content.

You don't have to form your database by only using phone numbers and emails, you can also communicate with your audience using advertising tools. Push notifications are browser-based SMS messages used to remind the audience about your product. Facebook is one of the most active social networks. Youtube is the audience with which you can communicate using video content. Collect all the people who visit your site using remarketing lists and communicate with them using advertisements when you need to show an advertisement to a specific person at a specific time.

Case 2. Community

Build your community. You should not be the lone voice for your product. Those who read your blog and watch your webinars should also speak for you. People are always asking for advice on good courses for digital marketing. If I don't have time to recommend our academy, people who know about us will. We have monitoring enabled on all social networks; we see every time we are mentioned. Your content can also give you people who will recommend you, even if they themselves never buy your product.

Case 3. PR

Content gives your company PR. When I was the director of development for the agency, it was difficult for me to communicate with journalists. I just said, «Write that we have a great agency,» but they would always ask me for something a little more descriptive. When you have a lot of content, you have many reasons to be published in various news resources. If you've done your research correctly, trade publications will immediately want to reprint your content. Our online conferences are large industry events that are important for the market, and it is not a sin to write about them in the media.

Every piece of content that you have produced (research, infographics, events, webinars) is a PR event. Use them wisely for communication, and you will be surprised how journalists will start asking you to comment on their news websites.

Case 4. Recognition

The fourth thing that content gives is awareness. Awareness is tied to the community, PR, and your brand advocates. When someone asks about you, people will talk about you or your product. This is what you need to be prepared for. Recognition has both positive and negative sides.

Case 5. Links

Without links, you won't get traffic from other sites and search engines. With content marketing, you can get good, natural links to your site. Therefore, use any excuse to post on a news resource, thematic community, forum, or platform that writes about your topic. This could include links from calendars, post releases, press releases, event reports, and reprints of your research and infographics.

Case 6. Employees

People may want to work for you by seeing the content you generate. When we first started, we had to explain to our employees who we are and what we are about during the interview process. Now future employees know all about us and can't wait to work with us.

Case 7. Partners

Content can be a vehicle for attracting partners. You will be able to meet and make friends with companies that you would never get to know otherwise. When we started to generate content and hold events, we invited speakers and looked for people who have a high position in the market. It was these people who helped us in many matters. The partners you find through content creation can become your friends and possibly business partners.

Case 8. Positive and negative feedback
There is no getting away from this. For every missing letter, you can get an angry comment on all your channels. After talking with book publishers, we realized that it is impossible to satisfy everyone. Critics are only one component of feedback and far from the most important. More often, people come to help your product do better. We all wear rose-colored glasses, and when we look at our product, it looks perfect. But when you get third-party feedback, you may find that there are many things you didn't notice. Constructive reaction to criticism makes your product incredibly powerful.

Case 9. Sales
Using content correctly and understanding who you are communicating with will help you receive stable sales growth. The content you create will attract people who will become your buyers. Remember that content is the kingmaker. When you have strong content, everything else will fall into place. Follow what you have read in this book, and I guarantee that you will start to see your business succeed and grow. Now get out there and get started!

www.ingramcontent.com/pod-product-compliance
Lightning Source LLC
Chambersburg PA
CBHW070241220526
45465CB00004B/1472